The Lifelong Learner:

How to Develop Yourself, Continually Grow, Expand Your Horizons, and Pursue Anything

By Peter Hollins,
Author and Researcher at
petehollins.com

Table of Contents

TABLE OF CONTENTS   5

CHAPTER ONE: FROM "COMFORT ZONE" TO "GROWTH ZONE"   7

CHAPTER TWO: PASSION AND MOTIVATION FOR LIFELONG PURSUITS   43

CHAPTER THREE: USING WOOP TO SET AND ACHIEVE YOUR GOALS   67

CHAPTER FOUR: SELF-EDUCATION BEGINS AND ENDS WITH QUESTIONS   85

CHAPTER FIVE: THE SACRED, LIFE-CHANGING HABIT OF READING   115

CHAPTER SIX: PERSONAL KNOWLEDGE MANAGEMENT AND THE LEARNING PROCESS   131

CHAPTER SEVEN: CREATE YOUR OWN PERSONAL SYLLABUS AND REFLECTIVE LEARNING   153

CHAPTER EIGHT: PASSIVE VERSUS ACTIVE LEARNING AND HOW TO CAPITALIZE   183

CHAPTER NINE: GAMIFICATION—FOR LEARNING, RETENTION, AND MOTIVATION   **209**

SUMMARY GUIDE   **227**

CHAPTER ONE: From "Comfort Zone" to "Growth Zone"

Humans have a startling tendency to gravitate toward the mundane, the monotonous, the known. It's very easy for us to get stuck in a rut. If we're not careful, we can find ourselves years into a job or a relationship that we loathe simply because it's comfortable. Comfort zones litter all aspects of our lives, but what exactly do they entail?

Judith Bardwick, a management theorist, used the term "comfort zone" in her 1991 work, Danger in the Comfort Zone. She postulates that the comfort zone is a behavioral state in which a person functions in an anxiety-free state, employing a limited set of behaviors to achieve a consistent level of performance, typically without any perception of risk.

Simply put, a comfort zone is an area where you feel safe and secure. It's familiar territory where you know what to expect. Think of it as the inside of your house. It's familiar, safe, and secure. The fear zone is the space just outside your house, where you feel a bit anxious and uncertain. Stepping outside of your house and out into the fear zone can be scary, but it's also how you will tackle new challenges, continuously learn new skills, and get things done.

As the fear zone is daunting and scary, it's natural to be a little anxious. But if you persevere and push through, you'll enter the learning zone. This is where your skills will blossom and obstacles will become opportunities for growth. When it comes to lifelong learning, having the courage to leave your comfort zone can open up new possibilities and opportunities. Stepping outside of our normal routines enables us to look at things with a different perspective and gain new insights, making us more flexible in both our thinking and approach to new situations.

Embracing the unfamiliar terrain of leaving our comfort zones also helps us build confidence and strengthen our resilience so that we can continue growing and learning for the rest of our lives. Eventually, this newfound knowledge learned means your comfort zone has expanded even further! Congratulations! You have now entered the growth zone. It's time to live your dreams, realize your aspirations, set new goals, and find your purpose. While it's comfortable to stick with what you know and just stay cuddled up in your comfort zone forever, that doesn't mean it's necessarily good for you.

Psychologists believe that spending too much time in our comfort zones can lead to boredom or stifle learning and personal growth (Leberman, Martin, 2002). Sometimes it's necessary to step outside of our comfort zones in order to learn new things or challenge ourselves. Abraham Maslow's (1943) theory of self-actualization posits that humans have an innate need to reach their full potential. This can only be done by challenging oneself and pushing beyond one's comfort zone. Therefore, to truly become self-actualized, we must be willing to take risks and face our fears.

When you think of a successful, intellectual, and talented individual, who comes to mind? Perhaps someone like Thomas Edison, the American inventor whose advancements to the light bulb made it a symbol of brilliance? But, despite being a very clever and talented guy, Edison famously tried ten thousand times to invent the light bulb. It was a lengthy, gradual process that required inquiry, perseverance, and hard effort.

According to renowned Stanford psychologist Carol Dweck in her book *Mindset*, it is not IQ, ability, or education that distinguishes successful people. It's their thinking, or how they tackle life's difficulties (Dweck, 2015). Her study separated two opposing belief systems: fixed versus growth mindsets.

People with a fixed mindset believe they have fixed amounts of each ability. To them, failure indicates inferiority, and criticism is a death blow to their self-esteem. In contrast, people with a growth mindset are adaptable. Any setbacks become opportunities for learning and growth (Dweck, 1999). Most of us have experienced some sort of setback in our lives. Maybe we didn't get the job we wanted, or our relationship ended unexpectedly.

Whatever the situation, we usually find a way to pick ourselves up and carry on. This ability to bounce back from adversity is known as resilience. While resilience is defined as performance recovery after degradation, antifragility is defined as performance gain when faced with adversity (Taleb, 2012). People who make it a habit to step outside their comfort zone are more equipped to deal with change and ambiguity, which leads to resilience and antifragility (Williams, 2022).

Psychologist Andy Molinsky has dedicated his career to understanding why people resist leaving their comfort zones, and how they can overcome that resistance. In his book *Reach*, he outlines several common psychological roadblocks that prevent people from taking risks and embracing new challenges. Some of them are feeling inauthentic in your pursuit of a dream, feeling like an imposter, fear of failure or embarrassment, uncertainty, the never-ending anxiety stirred by the unknown, and fear of being disliked.

These are all valid fears that come with the thought of leaving what is familiar. However, by acknowledging these psychological roadblocks, we can begin to overcome them and take steps toward leaving our comfort zones.

Use the 3 Cs to Achieve Escape Velocity

In his research, Molinsky discovered three techniques that people utilize to successfully venture outside of their comfort zones. He refers to these essential tools as the three Cs: conviction, customization, and clarity. Have you ever eaten a meal that was bland and unappealing until someone added a special ingredient that completely transformed it? Strong convictions are the secret ingredient of life. They are your core beliefs, such as altruism, generosity, gratitude, integrity, accountability, and perseverance. They are the qualities that give you a distinct spark and make you stand out. When you're certain that what you do and say matters and that what you provide is valuable to you and others, your energy transforms and you become persuasive and resilient. It provides you with a sense of security and allows you to focus on performing your best work since you know that everything you are doing matters to you.

Our minds are programmed to fearfully overreact to uncertainty. As uncertainty grows, the brain transfers control to the limbic system, which is where emotions like anxiety and fear are generated. If you are somebody with strong convictions, you don't give up when things get difficult. You're willing to take a bullet for the sake of your beliefs. You stand by them, never shifting blame. You might have observed some of these qualities in strong leaders. Their strong convictions can encourage others to publicly speak up and share their perspectives, even if what they say is difficult to hear.

According to Molinsky, the key to conquering your fears is to first develop a deep sense of your core values and beliefs. Without a sense of these, it's all too easy to talk yourself out of taking risks. Once you have conviction, however, the fear becomes manageable and you can start to take small steps outside your comfort zone. With each small success, you'll build confidence and eventually be able to take on bigger challenges.

Using the Three Cs: Conviction

A sense of conviction is important in many aspects of life. It can be the difference between success and failure, between happiness and misery. And yet, it is often difficult to develop a strong sense of conviction. So, how can we go about developing this core strength? Here are a few ideas.

First and foremost, it is important to have a clear understanding of what you believe in. What are your core values? What do you stand for? What is it that you aim to achieve by making this arduous journey outside your comfort zone? Once you have a good understanding of your own beliefs, it will be easier to stand up for them. Let's illustrate this with an example. Meet Barbara. She's a twenty-six-year-old about to embark on her first volunteer mission into a war-torn zone. Being an introvert, this task is very much out of Barbara's comfort zone. It is going to require a lot of energy and extra mental effort on her part, but she plans to proceed anyway.

How did Barbara come to this unwavering sense of purpose? Everyone has opinions and preferences, but a strong believer like Barbara does not develop their beliefs solely on their own desires or for their own benefit. A person who has strong personal convictions has considered the issues and the challenges, but instead of letting them hinder their growth, they see them as paths leading toward a purposeful life. They possess a growth mindset.

Barbara knows that ultimately she will end up making life-altering changes in people's lives and shower love where there is none. This conviction helps her stay grounded and expand her comfort zone more than ever before. Her comfort zone simply does not matter in the pursuit of her greater purpose and furthering her conviction.

Stepping outside your comfort zone can be a daunting prospect, but it is essential for personal growth, particularly when it comes to developing a strong sense of conviction. Taking risks and embracing uncertainty not only encourages Barbara to push the boundaries of her comfort zone, it also helps her strengthen her core beliefs and values. Being willing to explore unknown territories can ultimately lead to greater self-confidence in your convictions and an understanding that feeling uncomfortable at first doesn't necessarily mean something will end poorly. Rather, it can provide valuable insight that creates positive opportunities beyond what was previously thought possible.

Going into a war zone is not an easy decision and certainly not one you concoct within a span of a single night. Even going on a small casual vacation requires rigorous research and planning. Considering all perspectives, being open-minded, and welcoming cultures and customs different from our own require strength. Only if you are certain of your beliefs, goals, and grand purpose in life will you be able to develop an unwavering sense of conviction. Barbara knows what she wants. Do you?

Most of us have been in a situation where we question whether we made the right choice. It can be agonizing, second-guessing ourselves and wondering if we would have been better off choosing a different path. Uncertainty like this can be paralyzing, preventing us from making any decisions at all and making us lack conviction in anything we do. The key is to learn to trust your instincts and follow your convictions. When you make a decision from a place of deep faith, you are more likely to stick with it even when things get tough. Ultimately this is what will help you stay firmly planted in your growth zone while aiding you in remaining positive and hopeful for future challenges.

Additionally, it is very important to be prepared to face opposition. There will always be people who disagree with you, but if you are prepared for that opposition, it will be much easier to stay true to your convictions. It's critical to have personal convictions so we can resist being influenced by others' opinions or blindly following them. Someone without strong personal convictions will be unsure of themselves, uncertain, and susceptible to being misled.

It takes someone with strong moral convictions to stand up and declare "no" when the crowd chants, "Let's all be haters." Developing a strong sense of conviction is not easy, but it is definitely worth the effort. By taking the time to understand your own beliefs and values, by exposing yourself to new ideas, and by preparing for opposition, you can develop the inner strength that you need to stand up for what you believe in and forever flourish within your growth zone.

Using the Three Cs: Customization

In the world of fashion, customization is a process that allows you to take an existing piece of clothing and make it your own. You can add your own personal touches to it, like a special pocket for your cell phone, or you can completely change the look of it by adding a new collar or a sleeve. It's all about making the clothes you wear reflect your unique personality. And with so many different options to choose from, you're sure to find the perfect way to make your clothing truly yours.

Molinsky's customization refers to our ability to successfully adapt our behavior to our environments without losing ourselves in the process. Think of it as "fitting in" without completely "giving in." You're still you, just slightly altered (e.g., wearing your power suit, carrying your lucky charm, having some makeup on, wearing your favorite perfume, or arriving before everybody else on the day of your big speech) to trick yourself into feeling at home and to seamlessly blend into your environment. Whatever it is that we are doing or planning that requires us leaving our comfort zones can be altered, tweaked, or modified in a way that makes it feel more comfortable and natural and truly your own.

Whenever faced with a situation that requires you to step out of your comfort zone, try arranging the furniture in a way that brings you joy. For example, it's your wedding day and everything seems to be getting on your nerves. Getting the venue decorated and arranged in a way that brings you some semblance of normalcy and familiarity can help you get through the ceremony without having a breakdown. Pick out some of your favorite snacks as treats, or display photos with positive memories.

These things can help you build an environment that reflects your personality and lifts your mood, making you feel more comfortable. It doesn't have to be expensive or complicated; sometimes the simplest acts of self-care can make all the difference. Even something as simple as lighting a scented candle when you're inviting your significant other to your home for the first time, playing some music you enjoy, or wearing clothes that make you feel confident can help prepare you for whatever big challenge lies ahead. You can follow these guidelines and adapt them to whatever situation makes you want to run for the door.

Learning to adopt our behaviors to situations and surroundings can help us feel like we are within our own personal comfort zones. Depending on your situation, here are some tips and tricks that you can glean inspiration from. Let's say that you're deeply uncomfortable with walking into events with lots of people just staring at you as you walk by. Or you're uncomfortable walking into a classroom full of students with all eyes on you.

Social anxiety can be really debilitating and can stop people from wanting to leave their comfort zones. What I do in those situations is go earlier than everyone else. In college, I used to be the first person to enter the class and usually the last person to leave. This is a great way to reduce some of the anxiety you face in social situations and make the classroom feel like your own apartment—all comfortable and cozy. This is how I would customize my behavior to make what would otherwise be my fear zone feel like my personal comfort zone.

You know that feeling when you put on a really great outfit and you just feel like you can take on the world? Like you can conquer anything that comes your way? That's the feeling you get when you wear your power suit. Your power suit is the one that makes you feel strong and capable and ready to take on whatever the day throws at you. It's the one that gives you the confidence to walk into a room full of people and hold your head up high. It's the one that makes you feel like you can achieve anything.

So, when you put on your power suit, you are essentially putting on confidence, strength, and power. This is going to make that presentation feel just a bit more comfortable and natural so that you can make the leap into your fear zone without overwhelming your sympathetic nervous system too much. Molinsky suggests that by donning your power suit, you are customizing your behavior, and that is going to help your feet stay firmly planted within the growth zone. It'll be that anchor grounding you when all you want to do is run away.

Body language is a powerful thing. The way we carry ourselves can influence the way others perceive us, and it can also affect our own confidence levels. According to one study, one way to boost our confidence is to strike a so-called "power pose" before an important meeting or event (Carney et al., 2010). Power posing involves assuming a wide, open stance with your chest and head held high. This might mean standing with your hands on your hips or stretching your arms up over your head. The idea is that by taking up more space, we trick our brains into feeling more powerful. And when we feel more powerful, we're more likely to perform well in the meeting.

This is a great example of customizing your behavior (assuming a power pose) in order to make a situation (meeting) a little more comfortable and a little less daunting, more likely allowing you to perform well. So the next time you're feeling nervous before an important event, try striking a power pose for a few minutes. It just might help you ace that presentation!

Do you ever feel like you're just not having any luck? Like no matter what you do, things just don't seem to go your way? Well, maybe it's time to try carrying a lucky charm in your pocket. Now, I know what you're thinking. How can carrying a little trinket in your pocket possibly affect your luck? But hear me out. Just by having that little bit of positive energy with you throughout the day, you might be surprised at how things start to change. You might find yourself winning more arguments, getting picked for that big project at work, or finally landing that date with that cute person who has intrigued you. By carrying that little trinket, you are again customizing your behavior to make all these situations a little more comfortable and a little less daunting.

So next time you're feeling down on your luck, why not give it a try? Who knows, maybe that little charm will be exactly what you need to turn things around. Remember, your mindset is just as important as the physical actions you take to leave your comfort zone. If you do not have a positive, open-to-growth mindset, then you're likely to fall back into your comfort zone quickly. Consistent little healthy habits like these will help you hold on to hope and let go of your fears.

Using the Three Cs: Clarity

Clarity is gaining an objective, logical viewpoint of the difficulties you are facing. In other words, it's resisting the skewed and exaggerated thinking that so many of us do when faced with really stressful circumstances. For example, thinking that, "I'll never be able to submit this before the deadline!" without fully analyzing your situation (how much time you have left, how much progress you have already made) will let your anxiety about the challenge overwhelm you and keep you from ever leaving your comfort zone.

Thinking positively and eliminating negative thoughts can really improve clarity in our lives. Psychotherapist Tori Rodriguez says that acknowledging and challenging negative thoughts can lead to greater clarity and understanding of life. When you choose to focus on the positive, the intangible obstacles that stand between you and true understanding of a situation start to melt away. You become more mindful, open yourself up to new ideas, and realize what it is you actually want from life. This has great implications for lifelong learning, as this positive outlook on life drives you to be consistent in your pursuit of knowledge and learning new skills.

Destructive ruminations only serve to discourage us further, so if we remove these thoughts, we can find a renewed sense of purpose and hopefully clarity in our daily lives. Without understanding a situation, it's nearly impossible to truly learn anything from it. It's like having a jigsaw puzzle without the picture on it; you may have all the pieces but won't know how to put them together until you can see the bigger picture. To truly be successful in life, whether it's at work, school, or relationships, it helps to have a good understanding of ourselves and of the world around us.

This true understanding of life allows us to maintain lifelong learning while enjoying the journey along the way. That's the only way you can properly apply the knowledge and, most importantly, retain it for future use. It's like a domino effect; if the handling of one piece of information is not clear to you from the start, then your comprehension of subsequent pieces of related material is hampered as well. Without clarity, there can be little understanding of anything!

So, how do we start to challenge our negative thoughts and gain clarity over difficult situations? You need to start by looking at life's problems from a logical perspective, which can be key in finding a resolution. Such an outlook allows for a clearer understanding and for focusing on each individual issue as something to be understood and solved rather than simply accepted as inevitable or something too overwhelming to tackle.

Begin by incorporating mindfulness into your routine. It can help you view a situation or circumstance with a fresh perspective, allowing for more positive reflections and meaningful solutions to surface. Focus on slowly taking deep breaths and counting backward from ten. Count five things you can see, touch, and smell. This can help clear the mind and provide much-needed emotional grounding when faced with a difficult situation. Additionally, pay attention to your body's physical reaction to stress, as it can help you separate what you're feeling in the present moment from any irrational reactions or beliefs that may be contributing to the situation.

Not only does looking at things this way keep your emotions in check, but it also opens the door to creative solutions that would not be immediately seen by simply reacting emotionally or attempting to avoid issues entirely. Follow up by learning how to identify and dissect your distorted thoughts, as this is one of the main challenges you are going to face within the learning zone.

We all have irrational thoughts or beliefs from time to time. Especially when it involves venturing into the fear zone and leaving what is known behind. Maybe you're convinced that your boss is out to get you, or that you're not good enough for that new job, so you're not even going to try anyway. Irrational thoughts can be frustrating and even overwhelming when we are in the process of learning something new, but there are ways to deal with them.

The first thing that you need to do is simply acknowledge the thought and then let it go. For example, if you're thinking, "I'm not good enough," you can say to yourself, "I acknowledge that I'm feeling insecure right now, but I'm going to let that thought go." Other approaches include challenging the thought (e.g., "Is there evidence to support this?") or reframing it in a more positive light (e.g., "I'm feeling scared right now, but that's okay"), which can help us gain clarity and perspective.

Distorted thinking that results from a lack of clarity can also lead to frequent Automatic Negative Thoughts (ANTs). ANTs are, simply put, the negative thoughts that pop into our head automatically and unwantedly. We all have them from time to time (especially when outside of our comfort zones), but some of us get stuck in a cycle of ANTs, which can lead to feelings of depression and anxiety. ANTs usually take the form of "should" statements.

For example, "I should be thinner," "I should be better at this or smarter," or "I shouldn't have said that." They often involve beating yourself up for past mistakes or feeling like you're not good enough. Again, you need to acknowledge the thought ("I should be better at this"), then reframe it ("I am having the thought that I am not good enough for this task; I acknowledge that I am feeling insecure, but that is okay. Everyone feels inadequate at some point in their life") and then start to look for evidence for and against it.

This can help to break the cycle and give you a more realistic outlook on things and help you gain clarity. You can see how those kinds of thoughts could make you feel helpless and confine you to your comfort zones. Therefore, you must first acknowledge that you are thinking irrationally before you can gain clarity.

One other way to gain clarity over our negative thoughts is to practice self-reflection and examine our thoughts from an objective point of view. Questioning why we feel the way we do and becoming aware of potential distortions in our reasoning can also help us become more aware of our thought processes. Start by writing down your negative thoughts on a piece of paper and then drop them in an empty jar. Come back after a few days and read all the scrambled thoughts in there. Try asking yourself, "How do I feel about this now?" as you read through each one. Writing down negative thoughts or talking through them with a trusted friend or therapist are additional strategies that may help us develop healthier ways of engaging with our thought patterns.

Sometimes it's hard for us to recognize evidence contrary to our negative thoughts ourselves. Talking to someone else can help alleviate some of the anxiety we feel that comes with leaving our comfort zones.

Distorted thinking often distorts how individuals interpret the world around them, and this can have an impact on learning. For example, if someone believes they're not intelligent or capable of succeeding, this thought process can lead to behaviors that hinder learning opportunities. This could manifest as avoidance of challenging classes or activities, skipping school or homework assignments based on false beliefs about intelligence, or other self-sabotaging behaviors. It's important for those suffering from distorted thinking to be aware of these cognitive distortions and actively challenge their beliefs to succeed as lifelong learners.

So now we understand that staying in a comfort zone guarantees that you'll always be winning at life. There are no dragons to slay and no anxiety to make you want to hurl. For most people, it's the fear of failure that makes them want to stay put in their entirely risk-free comfort zones. But we now know that if you want to be anything worthwhile in life, you gotta break out of that cage. Venturing out into the fear zone and then subsequently into the learning zone can be scary, but fret not! For now, we move on to ways you can conquer that fear and forever thrive in the learning zone.

A Completely Rational Fear of Failure

"So, what do you think?" Ada asked her best friend, Emma. They were both perched on the edge of Emma's bed, looking at their laptops.

"I don't know," Emma said slowly. "It just feels like a lot of work."

Ada grinned. "Exactly! If it were easy, everyone would do it." She leaned back against the headboard and tossed her long hair over her shoulder. "Failure is a strength," she continued in a confident voice. "It means you're learning something new."

Emma stared at her for a moment before shaking her head and returning to her laptop screen. "Failure is a weakness and it means you can't do anything," she muttered under her breath.

We all view failures with our own unique perspectives and life-colored lens. People with a fixed mindset, such as Emma, believe that their abilities and intelligence are static. In contrast, people with a growth mindset, such as Ada, believe that their abilities can be developed through effort and perseverance. They see failures as opportunities toward lifelong learning and growth, and they are more likely to take risks and persevere in the face of adversity. Dweck's research has shown that people with a growth mindset are more likely to achieve success in school, work, and life.

We all experience failure in some capacity in our lives. But it doesn't mean that we have to stay stuck in a rut of negativity. It's important to remember that failure can be looked at as a learning experience and an opportunity for growth. Reframe it by thinking about what you can learn from the situation and use it to guide you.

A key part of lifelong learning is continuously updating your skillset, which not only keeps you relevant with current trends but also offers self-improvement possibilities. With continuous learning, failure becomes inevitable. Every time you try learning something new, you risk being a failure. This is why it is so important to conquer our failures if we want to continue learning and updating our skillset.

Anyone who's ever tried to make a chocolate bar at home knows that it's not as easy as it looks. In fact, it took Milton Hershey years of experimentation before he finally perfected his chocolate-making process. And yet, despite all his early failures, Hershey went on to become one of the most successful businessmen of his generation. So how did he do it?

For one thing, Hershey was never afraid to take risks. When he first started making chocolate, he was determined to find a way to mass produce his product. This required him to invest a great deal of money in new equipment and facilities. And while many other businessmen would have been content to stay small and play it safe, Hershey was willing to gamble everything on his vision.

He was incredibly relentless in pursuit of his goals. He continued to learn and improve his skill set. After multiple failed attempts, most people would have given up on making chocolate altogether. But Hershey never gave up hope that he could find a way to make delicious, affordable chocolate for everyone. His tenacity ultimately paid off, and his legacy continues to this day. So next time you bite into a Hershey's bar, remember the story of the man who made it all possible. Despite all the obstacles in his way, Milton Hershey never stopped believing in himself or his dreams. And that's something we can all learn from.

Elizabeth Day's book *How to Fail: Everything I've Learned from Things Going Wrong* is a funny, relatable, and ultimately uplifting look at the value of failure. Day starts off by recounting her own failures, from flunking out of acting school to getting fired from her first job. What becomes clear is that everyone experiences failure and that it's often those who have failed the most who end up being the most successful.

As Day puts it, "It is through our failures that we learn how to succeed." We all know the feeling of coming up short. Whether it's a failed test, a botched presentation, or a relationship that didn't work out, failure is always frustrating. But it's important to remember that every failure is an opportunity to learn and grow (Lattacher, Wdowiak, 2020).

Fearing failure is worse than failure itself because it will stop you from trying anything new in the first place. A study found that a stark fear of school failure can impair pupils' motivation to learn and can exert negative influence on attitudes toward learning (Michou et al., 2014). Students who developed a fear of failure early on in their lives were more likely to set and adopt goals just to validate their ego rather than for their own development and learning.

It is critical that we accept that there is always the risk that none of our efforts will be successful. Accepting that chance and making the most of it not only requires fortitude, but it also leads to richer and more rewarding lifelong learning experiences for those who do so. Now, let's move on to the five crucial steps, outlined by Dr. Theo Tsaousides, to conquer your failure.

Steps to Conquer Your Failure

Do you ever feel like you're not good enough? Like you're just not cut out for success? You might be suffering from a fear of failure. The fear of failure is a type of anxiety that can prevent us from taking risks and pursuing our learning goals. It can make us feel like we're not good enough or that we'll never be able to achieve our dreams. The good news is, you're not alone. The fear of failure is common, and it's something you can overcome. The first thing you have to do is:

Redefine Failure as a Discrepancy

Start by clearly defining what failure means to you. What does failure mean to you? Losing heart? Never pursuing your objectives? Not getting the intended result? Not getting results within the anticipated time frame? It's important to think about this question and its subsequent answer since failure is the object of your fear and anxiety and the main obstacle holding you back. True failure is when a person is so afraid of failure that they won't even try! As these quotes so beautifully put it:

"It is impossible to live without failing at something unless you live so cautiously that you might as well not have lived at all, in which case you have failed by default." –JK Rowling

"Children have a lesson adults should learn, to not be ashamed of failing, but to get up and try again. Most of us adults are so afraid, so cautious, so 'safe,' and therefore so shrinking and rigid and afraid that it is why so many humans fail. Most middle-aged adults have resigned themselves to failure." –Malcolm X

We all know what it feels like to fail. Whether it's a bad grade on a test, a missed opportunity, or something bigger, failure can sting. But what if we looked at failure differently? Instead of seeing it as the end of the road, what if we saw it as simply a discrepancy between our expectations and reality? When we redefine failure in this way, it becomes much less daunting. After all, every day we experience discrepancies. It's just part of life. It is when we embrace this mindset that we learn to see failures as simply another step on the road to learning something extraordinary. So next time you face a setback, remember that it's not the end of the world. It's just a discrepancy, and you're one step closer to your goal.

Distinguish between Real and Imagined Threats

It can be tough to know whether a threat is real or imagined. Oftentimes our minds can play tricks on us, magnifying innocuous situations into full-blown scares. So how can you tell the difference between a real and imagined threat? Start by paying attention to your body's physical response. Are you sweating, shaking, or having trouble catching your breath? These are all signs that your body is preparing for fight-or-flight mode. If there's no clear reason for these symptoms, it's likely that you're experiencing anxiety or an imagined threat rather than a real threat.

For example, somebody with a fear of public speaking might start to feel anxious weeks in advance about giving a presentation even though they haven't been asked to speak yet. Or somebody who's afraid of flying might avoid booking a vacation because they're worried about the plane ride. In these cases, the anxiety is disproportionate to the actual threat and there is little to no threat to your survival.

On the other hand, if you decide to give a presentation in front of a pride of lions on that vacation you finally booked, then you probably should listen to your body's fight-or-flight response, as the threat you are now facing is very real. The lions are not interested in the stats you are quoting; they only want to eat you.

Failure fear by definition incorporates imagined dangers. The fear is real, but the threat isn't. For now, the threat is your prediction, a fantasy of how you think a situation is going to pan out. However, your fear isn't illogical or unjustified, just premature and unneeded. Analyze it and ask yourself whether the threat is based on fact or opinion. If you're unsure about something, it's always best to err on the side of caution and take a closer look. Additionally, there are plenty of ways to deal with anxiety, whether it's real or imagined.

Talking to a therapist can be helpful in getting to the root of your anxiety and learning how to manage it. Exercises like yoga and meditation can also be calming, and sometimes all you need is a distraction; so go ahead and binge-watch that new show on Netflix! Whatever method you choose, don't let your fear stop you from learning and discovering something new.

Create Promotion Rather than Prevention Goals

Most of us are pretty good at setting goals for ourselves. Whether it's losing/gaining weight, quitting smoking, or working out more, we usually have a pretty good idea of what we want to achieve. However, when it comes to health and wellness, many of us default to "prevention" goals rather than "promotion" goals. In other words, we focus on avoiding bad outcomes rather than actively pursuing good ones.

For example, rather than setting a goal to walk ten thousand steps a day, we might set a goal to not sit for more than thirty minutes at a time. While there's nothing inherently wrong with prevention goals, research suggests that promotion goals are more effective in promoting lasting behavior change, and a predominantly promotional focus—a mentality in which people place more emphasis on progress and achieving goals than on security and doing chores—is a key precursor to adaptability, learning, and creativity (Higgins,

1997, 1998; Camacho, Higgins, 1999). That's because promotion goals are concrete and actionable, while prevention goals tend to be vague and easy to rationalize away.

Moreover, sticking to promotion goals prevent stagnation in a particular position or a career or a learning path that can lead to boredom and potentially put a halt on progress. Developing an attitude of continuous growth toward learning not only sets you up for success in the workplace but encourages healthy personal development as well.

One strategy for removing failure fear from the equation is to reframe prevention goals as promotion goals. So, the next time you catch yourself setting prevention goals such as "I hope I don't lose my job" or "I don't want my boyfriend to break up with me," try to replace your thoughts with anticipating more positive outcomes rather than focusing on the negatives. Try setting some promotion goals instead: "I am going to work extra hard and aim for a promotion" or "I want to deepen my relationship with my boyfriend."

Prevention goals are often created out of a fear of failure, which can distort our priorities, undermine our efforts, and dampen our learning efforts.

Expect a Good Outcome but Do Not Become Attached to It

Most of us are attached to something: our things, our relationships, our memories, the desired outcomes of our goals, etc. And while attachment isn't necessarily a bad thing, it can become problematic when we become too attached to something. When we're attached to an outcome, we're focused on the end result rather than the journey. We become fixated on what we want, and we lose sight of what's really important. We start seeing any form of deviation from our initially envisioned outcome as a failure.

This can lead to frustration, disappointment, and even depression. So how do we avoid becoming too attached? The key is to expect a good outcome but not to become attached to it. Have faith that things will work out, but don't put your entire happiness on the line. Start by re-evaluating and adjusting the outcomes you expected.

For example, let's say your boss passed you up on that big promotion that you were so sure you were going to get. If you attach yourself to the outcome you expected (promotion), you will weave yourself into the dark web of discrepancies and convince yourself that you are obviously failing at life ... which couldn't be further from the truth!

Be open, be flexible, and customize the outcome accordingly. Sometimes what you perceive as a failure is actually a blessing in disguise. This outcome was not desirable, but that doesn't mean it cannot help you re-evaluate your life choices. You can start focusing on developing your ideas, double down on your efforts, and just enjoy the journey rather than worry about things outside of your control. Focus on what you can control, for that is the only thing that truly matters. To quote Taylor Swift, "Everything you lose is a step you take." And indeed, it is.

Reevaluating and revising your goals can help you overcome your fear of failure. We should evaluate our success based on the amount of thought and effort we put in rather than the outcome. If we limit ourselves to the outcome, we will never be able to improve or develop our skill sets.

You Are Strong and You Can Prevail

Fear of failure is not motivated by the difficulties ahead or the work required. It is about the consequences of our failure. We are not terrified of the job we must perform, but of the remote possibility that our effort may not be good enough to produce results that meet our expectations.

To further thwart the fear of failure, start by acknowledging and distinguishing the consequences of failure that you're most afraid of. Then, discuss your ability to overcome those consequences. At this stage, it is important to build enough confidence to deal with the outcomes instead of taking yourself out altogether in fear of negative consequences.

Here are some questions you can ponder the answers to:

- Which of these outcomes/consequences scares you the most?
- What effect will they have on you? Are they merely annoying or potentially fatal? Will they simply make you uncomfortable, or will they deeply and irreversibly harm you?
- How rapidly will you progress? Are the impacts irreversible or reversible? Are they fleeting, or do they last forever?
- How well can you deal with them? Can you exert damage control, or will you hide and vanish?

I'll illustrate this using my own life as an example. Whenever I dread an outcome, a consequence, a result, I take my notepad and write down my fears, my insecurities, and what I believe are my core strengths that will help me in overcoming this numbing feeling.

Everyone experiences fear at some point in their lives. Whether it's fear of public speaking, fear of heights, or fear of failure, it's a normal and healthy emotion. However, when fear begins to interfere with our ability to live our lives, it becomes a problem.

For me, the consequences of failing scare me the most. I'm afraid of not being good enough, of disappointing my family and friends, and of never reaching my full potential. However, I'm also aware that these are all risks that come with any venture. And while I can't control the outcome, I can control my own effort and attitude. So while the thought of failure still scares me, I know that I have the strength to overcome it.

Finally, what makes us fearless is not the absence of fear, but the certainty that we can handle the consequences of our actions. That is what makes people fearless, and it may also help you overcome your fear of failure.

Chapter Takeaways

- Embracing the uncharted terrain of leaving your comfort zones aids in the development of confidence and resilience, allowing you to continue developing and learning for the rest of your life. This acquired understanding eventually means that your comfort zone has increased even further and you are now in the growth zone.
- Psychologist Andy Molinsky has dedicated his career to understanding why people resist leaving their comfort zones, and how they can overcome that resistance using three Cs: conviction, customization, and clarity. You must develop strong convictions, which are your core beliefs, such as altruism, generosity,

gratitude, integrity, accountability, and perseverance.
- Customization relates to your ability to successfully adjust your behavior to your surroundings without losing yourself in the process. Consider it "fitting in" without fully "giving in." You're still you, just slightly altered (e.g., wearing your power suit, carrying your lucky charm, etc.) to trick yourself into feeling at ease and easily blending into your surroundings. Lastly, you must have clarity, which is obtaining an objective, rational perspective on the problems you are facing. By challenging your negative thoughts, you can gain a clearer picture of your challenges.
- Leaving your comfort zone and facing new challenges will sometimes guarantee failure. However, it is important to remember that every failure is an opportunity for us to learn and grow. Therefore, define failure as a discrepancy to help reframe your mindset. Start by looking at it as a discrepancy between your expectations and reality. Determine if the threat is real or imagined by evaluating your body's physical response.
- Additionally, create promotion goals rather than prevention goals to stay focused on what's important. This development of a goal-oriented growth mindset toward learning not only prepares you for success in your chosen profession, but it also promotes healthy personal development. Expect a good

outcome but do not become attached to it, so you can enjoy the journey. Have faith in the outcome, but don't put your entire happiness on the line.

CHAPTER TWO: Passion and Motivation for Lifelong Pursuits

Achieving something that once seemed impossible is such an amazing feeling, and learning to do so involves stepping out of your comfort zone. Sure, it can be intimidating at first—a lot of us have experienced failure or had difficulties in the past and aren't eager to face it head-on. But understanding that growth comes from pushing yourself beyond your limits and embracing challenges will go a long way on your journey.

Instead of dwelling on your inability to learn and grow, aim for progress by re-framing failures as just part of the process—it shows that you're trying! As you move ahead and start searching for your ultimate passion, you can look back with pride, knowing that you took those initial steps forward yourself.

But how do we initiate that internal drive to pursue what is most important to us? How do we ignite our intrinsic motivation to reach our passions?

As a young, curious wide-eyed girl, Jane loved nothing more than exploring the world around her. She was constantly asking questions and trying to figure out how things worked. Nothing could dampen her thirst for knowledge and learning new things. Her parents were always impressed by her intelligence and creativity, and they did their best to encourage her natural curiosity.

One day, when Jane was about ten years old, she came across a book on physics in her parents' library. She quickly became fascinated by the concepts it described, the beguiling images of the cosmos, theories on time travel and time dilation, the quirkiness of quarks, the peculiar behavior of matter and light. She spent hours reading about the laws of motion and energy. Soon enough, physics became Jane's favorite subject in school. She loved learning about the universe and discovering new ways to understand it.

Throughout high school and college, Jane continued to study physics with enthusiasm. She even started doing research in quantum mechanics, which was one of the most complex fields of physics. But no matter how hard she tried, she couldn't seem to break into that field as a researcher.

Finally, after years of frustration, Jane decided to take a different approach. Instead of focusing purely on her own ambitions, she started helping other students learn physics. She expanded her skillset and found that she enjoyed teaching just as much as researching, and eventually became a professor at a major university. Jane's story is a great example of how intrinsic motivation can turn us into lifelong learners hellbent on discovering our true passion.

We all have experienced intrinsic motivation at some point; think about a time when you lost track of time because you were completely absorbed in what you were doing. Maybe it was painting, playing an instrument, reading a book, or organizing your closet. Intrinsic motivation is often driven by a sense of satisfaction, pride, or achievement.

Alternatively, it could be something you find enjoyable or fun. For example, many people are intrinsically motivated to exercise because they enjoy the endorphin rush that comes with it. By staying curious, intrinsically motivated, and following her instincts, Jane ended up finding something that made her incredibly happy.

Intrinsic motivation is essential for lifelong learning. This type of motivation fuels the desire to keep learning and exploring new things, even if it's outside your comfort zone. It's great when extrinsic rewards like grades or a promotion comes along, but in the end, if you don't have that passion for learning inside you, then it can be difficult to stay committed over time.

Passion, according to life coach Susanna Newsonen, is "a sort of positive energy that you can experience in multiple areas of your life." The most common interpretation of passion in organizational studies is teleological, implying a powerful, purposive motivation to achieve an end goal (Linstead, Brewis, 2007).

It is the joy and the internal drive Jane felt when she'd immersed herself in quantum mechanics. It is the joy you feel when you pick up your favorite racket, your favorite book, your beloved guitar, or your paintbrush. This joy bubbles forth from unbridled curiosity fueled by intrinsic motivation. Jane's source of inspiration that sowed the very first seeds of her passion came from within. Intrinsic motivation is internal.

It's when you do something because you want to, not because you have to. You're driven by a personal interest or enjoyment in the task itself. Karen Putz explained the five stages of passion and how knowing where you are can help you hone and develop them further. I will also explain how intrinsic motivation plays a key role in each stage.

In the C.L.E.A.R. path to passion, the first stage we have is curiosity. Consider Jane's love for asking questions and hiding in her parents' library. This is the birthplace of your passion. Then comes learning and enthusiasm—Jane's desire and enthusiasm to learn anything and everything she could about quantum mechanics. This is the stage that ignites and increases intrinsic motivation and elicits enthusiasm, thus allowing significant connections to take place, sparking Jane's interest and her curiosity (Hennessey, 2015).

Along comes awareness; this is where you will commit to forever keep your passion alive and keep it flowing. If we look at Jane's example once again, we'll notice how she kept herself intrinsically motivated and pursued her passion in all its forms until she found a fit that worked for her. The trick here is to never stop learning and letting your passion grow. Lastly, we have recognition; this is where people take one look at your life and know how your passion makes you stand out. For example, Jane will forever stand out as a quantum physicist because that is what defines her.

Jane's curiosity about how the world worked on a subatomic level was what set the wheels of discovering her true passion in motion. Her joy was understanding the universe on a deeper level than most of us. Intrinsic motivation was the driving force in reaching her goals. It was what created the curiosity, the passion, the desire, and the ambition to pursue learning what she loved most.

People like Jane, who are driven by intrinsic motivation, find their work meaningful because they dedicate themselves, give their all, and solve difficult and important problems. These people are genuinely motivated by a desire to learn and grow, to find meaning, and most importantly joy, that contributes to a greater good. Extrinsic motivation, on the other hand, is our desire to engage in an activity in order to obtain rewards or avoid punishments.

In other words, we are motivated by an activity's instrumental value (Ryan, Deci, 2000). Extrinsic aspirants regard financial wealth, physical beauty, and notoriety or celebrity as more significant or worthy aims in life (Deci et al., 2017). Personal growth, community, and meaningful relationship goals, on the other hand, fall under the category of intrinsic ambitions, which are more likely to predict positive outcomes such as work satisfaction and wellbeing (Deci et al., 2017).

According to a Deloitte study from 2014, 87 percent of Americans felt unable to deliver their full potential at work owing to a lack of passion (Su, 2019). A lack of passion is a direct consequence of a lack of intrinsic motivation. If there's no internal motivation, there's no curiosity. If there's no curiosity, there's no drive, no enthusiasm, no desire to learn or pursue something new.

Because intrinsic motivation comes from inside, a sense of fascination with life and the learner's world is highly valued and necessary. The intrinsic learner prioritizes a sense of accomplishment and mastery. They are not dependent on other people's thoughts, and they know there are things they can't fully control (Gillard, Gillard, Pratt, 2015). Intrinsically motivated people are lifelong learners, as they never tire of learning more and more about what they love.

Nurturing and maintaining intrinsic motivation are lifelong skills that students must develop in the twenty-first century, where they must independently obtain and analyze vast volumes of information. It is the responsibility of educators to employ numerous motivational tactics in order to impact a student's ability to find their passions. In the context of lifelong learning, intrinsic motivation is far more powerful than extrinsic motivation.

According to research, pupils who are intrinsically motivated to study perform better academically and finish more years of education than those who are not intrinsically motivated (Korb, 2012). Several studies have repeatedly shown that intrinsic drive leads to greater persistence, psychological well-being, and performance (Deci, Ryan, 2008). So, how do you go about increasing your intrinsic motivation?

And discover your lifelong passion? Let's move on to discuss some ways you can do this.

How to Increase Intrinsic Motivation in Your Life

The self-determination theory (SDT) of motivation proposed by Deci and Ryan (2008) assumes that "people are by nature active and self-motivated, curious and interested, vital and willing to succeed since success itself is personally pleasant and rewarding." Circumstances and settings, on the other hand, can leave us "alienated and robotic, or passive and dissatisfied." But there's good news for you. You have the power to change your circumstances for the better!

Satisfying Our Basic Psychological Needs

The three fundamental psychological requirements identified by the SDT, according to Susan Fowler (2019), are "foundational to all human beings and our ability to flourish." Each one must be met for engaged, passionate people to do excellent work in any field. You can start by building supportive environments that encourage autonomy, competence, and relatedness, resulting in increased intrinsic motivation all around.

Creating an environment that promotes autonomy (the capacity of a person to pursue their own values and interests) might sound daunting, but it can be done with a few simple steps. First, it's important to find ways to build trust; this could include giving employees more freedom in their job roles and tasks. You should also ensure that teams have access to resources, ideas, and the level of support they need to succeed.

Additionally, providing autonomy requires a leader who is willing to listen to employees and their ideas, including how things are done or changes that can be made. Last but not least, autonomy builds when employees feel respected for the decisions they make. By setting up these key foundations for success, your team will thrive in an atmosphere of autonomy.

Achieving success often comes down to having individual goals, and those goals need to be defined if they are going to drive an individual's progress. While it is important to strive for these objectives, how one chooses to reach them is paramount. Taking the "carrot method" of attainment, with incentives like rewards and social recognition, can help frame goals as essential while avoiding pressure.

This allows people more autonomy in how they decide to pursue their ambitions, which encourages intrinsic motivation rather than just doing something because they have to. Ultimately, goal setting can be an effective tool in anyone's success story; you just need to present it in a way that makes people excited to take on the challenges instead of feeling obligated.

Developing a sense of relatedness to others is an essential part of living a meaningful life. You need to take the time to strengthen your relationships and deepen the connections you have with others. Frequently ask yourself and others around you, "Are you happy in life?" "Does your heart yearn for more?" Then ask yourself the same questions. One important step is to connect work with a higher cause, such as political, moral, spiritual, or corporate values.

It can help give you greater motivation and reward for the work you do. It's important to identify how you feel about what you are doing. Being aware of emotions involved in our day-to-day activities can contribute to deeper levels of relatedness; it's far easier to have strong relationships when we can empathize and understand the motivations of those around us. Embracing many aspects of life together leads to richly connected interactions that result in strong relationships and more fulfilling lives all around.

Competence (entails the need to believe you are capable of reaching desired results) is essential when it comes to building your passion. You need to have both the right skills for your chosen task and the opportunity to show them off.

Start by making sure there are ample learning resources available. With today's technology, there are more learning resources available than ever before. From online classes to YouTube tutorials, there are so many ways to learn new skills and get access to valuable knowledge. And it's not just the internet that can provide resources; libraries still offer an incredible selection of textbooks and other reference materials for those who prefer more traditional ways of studying.

It can be so easy to get caught up in chasing results and measuring our efforts based on the outcomes. Set learning goals to focus on the building blocks that are needed for success instead of simply looking at the end product. This approach will encourage you to reflect on your progress and adjust your strategy as needed. Let's look at John's journey to help you understand the importance of setting up learning goals.

John had always been a bit of a slacker when it came to school. He would usually do just enough to get that B, without pushing himself too hard. This semester, however, he decided to set some healthy learning goals for himself. He wanted to make sure he was actually learning and not just focusing on getting a B to make his parents happy.

To start off, John created a study schedule for himself and stuck to it religiously. He made sure to take breaks and allow himself time to relax, but overall he was really proud of how well he was doing. His grades went from B's to A's, and he started feeling more confident in his abilities.

The best part was that John was actually enjoying his classes now! He found that he was learning a lot more than he ever had before. And the most amazing part? He could still goof off with his friends on the weekends without feeling guilty. Setting healthy learning goals for himself turned out to be the best decision John ever made! Focusing on learning rather than results made all the difference in John's life. Stop focusing on achievements and start focusing on your needs and your growth instead.

Engage in Great Storytelling and Find Your One Sentence

Everyone loves a good story. Whether it's a thrilling adventure tale, a heartwarming slice of life, or a side-splitting comedy, there are few things more enjoyable than getting lost in the power of a great storyteller. From classic folktales passed down through generations to the latest binge-worthy show on Netflix, the art of telling through words has been around for centuries.

How we feel about what we do is less about the activity itself and more so about how we perceive it. For example, I, too, sometimes get plagued by thoughts of how mundane, monotonous, and pointless my job is. But then I pause and think about how many lives I save every single day deep from within the throes of mental illness. If some of my patients didn't have me, they'd have nobody. Similarly, try to look at the grand scheme of things and trust the process. Does an artist give up working on his painting after the first stroke? Does a musician give up after his first lyric? Does a doctor give up when his patient passes away? Does an astronaut stop searching for intelligent life just because the probability of life outside of our universe is so low? No! They know that all of this is going to be worth the masterpiece they create/find in the end.

They believe in their purpose, and they have narratives surrounding their passions. In fact, that is exactly how you know if something is it for you. When what you do is lyrical, it's beautiful, meaningful, and full of tales and adventure for you; know that you have found your passion! Perspective truly is everything.

If I asked you to sum up your life with one sentence only, would you be able to do it? You'd be surprised how many people would reply with, "I have no idea who I am." Which is okay, most of us don't. We have many goals and aspirations spread across our lifetime that can make it difficult to answer questions such as these.

Daniel Pink, in his 2018 book *Drive*, challenges us to regain focus and clearly define our mission. He invites us to define a statement that sums up our lives. As an example, he provides us a sentence that might be Abraham Lincoln's: "He preserved the Union and freed the slaves."

What's yours?

To make it easier, think about how you want to be viewed by others, or your top values and interests, and weave those together into one succinct statement. Think about your goals and ask yourself: "Am I closer today to achieving my goals?" "Is there something I need to do so that I move in the right direction?" "How can I improve my strategy?" Your statement doesn't have to be anything overly complex; just remember to make it meaningful to you so that it will resonate with you and anyone else who reads it.

It could be something as simple as "I am a clinical psychologist and I help save lives every day" or "I am an artist connecting people when words fail." That way, when someone asks you to tell them a bit about yourself, you'll have something great to share!

How Can I Increase My Intrinsic Motivation so that I Learn Better?

You need to engage yourself in accordance with your basic psychological needs to help boost your intrinsic motivation. Ask yourself the following questions:

- Do you have some control over when and how you do your work (Autonomy)?
- Is this task interesting, unique, and conducive to mastery (Competence)? Or is it mindless, monotonous, and rote learning?
- Do you understand the significance or aim of this piece of work? For example, it could lead to something more advanced or a larger piece of work. So they need to understand why you are doing what you are.

Give yourself the chance to explore your own interests and discover something new! Setting aside some time for yourself to work on an idea or project of your choice will help nurture autonomy, creativity, and problem-solving skills. It's also important to know how to offer yourself praise because the way we often do it is extremely damaging to our intrinsic motivation.

For example, you might've heard your mama say, "If you get an A on this test, you can have pizza for dinner." You end up studying hard not because you genuinely want to or enjoy it; you'll do it for the pizza. This can damage creativity and intrinsic motivation.

Therefore, instead of praising yourself for being smart, praise your hard work and good planning. Let's go back to John's example and how he set up healthy learning goals for himself. He shouldn't be praised because he received an A. We need to focus on the specifics here. His ability to create a healthy schedule and goals should be praised. His ability to persevere and be consistent should be applauded. These are the qualities that made him stand out, and they should be praised.

It is important that kids (and adults who are learning) get credit for the challenges they take on and the work they do, rather than just focusing on hearing praise when they have achieved a desired result Only give yourself compliments when you have a good reason. Don't praise everything; instead, recognize extra effort and be sincere. Praise is a powerful way to motivate people, but if it's not done right, it can cancel out a lot of the good it does.

How to Ignite Your Intrinsic Motivation to Reach Your Passion

While it is critical to balance both intrinsic and extrinsic drive, an inner motive is frequently more difficult to find. We live in a world full of external incentives, from money to celebrities to job advancements, and it's easy to lose sight of our internal objective. Intrinsic motivation is a critical component of success. It is what enables you to build your passions and ambitions based on you rather than extraneous influences.

Having fulfilled the requirements of autonomy, competence, and relatedness, we now recall the five stages of passion discussed earlier (the C.L.E.A.R. path). The first stage we had was curiosity. Keep in mind that without autonomy, there will be no curiosity because what's the point in chasing it, really? That's surely not how you're going to pass that class. Feeding your curiosity is one of the finest methods to help you build on your passion.

Curiosity generates new challenges, new experiences, and personal growth, all of which contribute to success. What piques your curiosity? What is something you've always wanted to study or do but haven't gotten around to doing? Todd Henry, author of *The Accidental Creative and Louder Than Words*, advises on an exercise called the notables when assisting clients in discovering their secret passion. He suggests writing down your answers to the following questions:

What angers you? What makes you cry? What gives you hope?

"I'm talking about compassionate anger," Henry clarifies, as opposed to raging road rage. "Compassion implies 'to suffer together.' What gives you sympathetic rage? What do you go through and immediately think, 'Ugh! Someone should do something about it!'"

According to Henry, "that someone is probably you, and now you've stumbled into a clue to the creative passion that will fuel your most important work." Here, you have to indulge in your curiosity to find creative ways you can approach this. For example, when I am coming back from work and I see all the homeless sprawled across the sidewalks, I think to myself, "Ugh! Someone needs to figure out how to eradicate homelessness for good!" I haven't yet figured out if that someone is supposed to me, but it's definitely something to think about. Maybe my profession as a psychologist is an echo of that passion? Passion to ease someone else's pain however I can? Who knows!

Things that affect us emotionally are excellent indicators of constructive passion. Is there something that moves you deeply? Is there something that fills you with unbridled hope? Is there something that only you can find value in, while others surrounding you don't necessarily understand it?

Maybe it's something about working with children? Maybe it's music and you want to be a songwriter one day. Maybe it's art, maybe it's writing, maybe it's graphic design. If you notice a consistent theme across things that result in a deep emotional impact, maybe it's something you'd want to pursue. Remember, some of the greatest ideas and inventions we have today came from people who saw diamonds in coal long before anyone else could see them.

Moreover, you can also think about the following questions suggested by Karen Putz. This can help you self-evaluate. Ponder your past: "What was a major moment of joy in your past?" "Who were you with?" "What were you doing?" "Where were you?" Explore the present: "When you're standing in line at the DMV, waiting at the dentist office, or sitting in a boring meeting, can you note what thoughts/memories/wishes pop up?"

The answers to these questions will serve as clues to your passions. Contemplate the future: "What are you putting off for the future?" "What's on your "someday" list? ("Someday, when I have money, when the kids are old enough, when I retire," etc.) "What do you dream about?" After identifying your delayed intentions, create an action plan to start in the here and now, not someday.

Now that we have done a significant amount of homework cultivating and igniting our intrinsic motivation, kept our curiosity burning, answered lots of questions about what sparks joy within us, it's time to actually inventory your talents and get to the nitty gritty and start your search for your passion.

Begin by taking **detailed inventory of your talents**. Everyone has something they are incredibly good at, even if they will never believe it. Ask yourself if there is something that you particularly enjoy doing or have a special knack for? It can be anything that brings you joy. For example, you might love to paint, draw, write music, take pictures, or write poems. You might have a special skill like carpentry or pottery, or you might be our upcoming Amaury Guichon, who is a French-Swiss chef with a passion for creating edible chocolate sculptures. Seriously, the sheer joy on that man's face as he fashions those incredible pieces of art is just otherworldly and beautiful.

So, in case something isn't making you as happy as chocolate makes Guichon happy, then it probably isn't your passion. Remember, intrinsic motivation increases and ignites when something sparks joy deep within you. Your curiosity should unearth that source of joy in order to allow you to develop your passion.

Also, pay attention to anyone **who makes you super annoyed or jealous**. Sometimes those feelings stem from an unmet desire that we have long buried. Is there someone with a hobby who annoys you? Perhaps someone who travels a lot? Is the truth behind that annoyance a yearning for similar circumstances and freedom? Perhaps this was something that you always wanted for yourself but never had the courage to pursue?

Go back to your childhood and think about what you loved doing the most. Most children are sure of exactly what they want and what would make them the happiest before adults infect them with their own ideas of what they think a child should love. Thinking back to my childhood often brings a vivid image of me playing make-believe with the neighborhood children for hours on a sunny Saturday afternoon. We would let our imaginations run wild as we turned the playground into an alternate universe where the slide was an ancient temple and the swing set represented a magical forest. We could be heroes or villains, monarchs or outlaws in another realm of life that seemed far more exciting than school or chores. I can still vividly recall how much joy these adventures brought to my youthful heart and soul!

Ultimately it was these adventures that led me to discover my passion for writing stories about my travels across the world. These stories brought me the same joy that I felt as a kid running around wildly across that playground so many years ago. Perhaps there's something long buried from your childhood too? If you have been looking for a sign to get that musty old guitar out of your garage or drag out that easel lying in the attic, this is it. DO IT NOW! You'll notice how you lose track of time and portal to a time when you were the happiest and felt the freest you have ever been.

When I write, I don't experience time as I normally would. I have to drag myself away to attend to things that I'd rather not be doing. When you find joy in doing something, you'll never get tired of it.

Most importantly, **see your passion hunt as a fun and joyful adventure**! During group therapy, I observe so many of my clients put undue pressure on themselves to find their passion. While I do believe that it's essential we all have that one thing that lights us up with child-like wonder, it's equally important that we don't feel pressured to locate it. You have to gradually open yourself up to experiencing new things; don't take the journey of self-discovery too seriously.

You will be learning and growing, so don't be afraid to make mistakes! Play and adventure should be crucial aspects of this hunt. You will fall, you will fail, and you will get hurt, but in the end, this is all going to be worth it, for you will have found a treasure of a passion that very few are lucky to call their own. Pay attention to what makes you happy, what lights you up, what you yearn more for. Once something sparks joy, hold on to it, make time for it, and feel how it transforms your life.

Chapter Takeaways

- Intrinsic motivation is essential for lifelong learning and fuels the desire to keep learning

new things, even if it's outside your comfort zone. This innate internal drive is what fuels your passion. Passion itself is a positive energy that you can experience in multiple areas of your life. The most common interpretation of passion in organizational studies is teleological, implying a powerful, purposive motivation to achieve an end goal.
- Intrinsic motivation comes from within and is when you do something because you want to, not because you have to. You're driven by a personal interest or enjoyment in the task itself. For example, learning to bake simply because you enjoy it.
- There are three fundamental psychological requirements identified by the self-determination theory (SDT) that are "foundational to all human beings and our ability to flourish. These requirements, which must be met for engaged, passionate people to do excellent work in any field, are autonomy (the capacity of a person to pursue their own values and interests), competence (the need to believe you are capable of reaching desired results), and relatedness (a sense of connection with others).
- To increase intrinsic motivation, it is first important to build supportive environments that encourage these things. It's important to create an environment that fosters trust and encourages healthy discourse. Second, focus on learning goals rather than results-based goals. Learning happens regardless of

whether you achieve your desired results. Lastly, connect work with a higher cause or something that gives your work greater meaning.
- Intrinsic motivation contributes to success by enabling you to build your passions and ambitions based on you rather than extraneous influences. To ignite intrinsic motivation, consider what angers or moves you emotionally, what piques your curiosity, or what you loved doing in childhood. Work on your perspective and find the one sentence that perfectly defines you.
- Take inventory of your talents and look for things that bring you joy. If something annoys or makes you feel envious, there may be an unmet desire buried there that could be worth pursuing as a passion project.

CHAPTER THREE: Using WOOP to Set and Achieve Your Goals

Setting goals is key to any form of learning and personal growth. By setting goals, you can focus your energies in the right direction, as well as see clearly how far you have come and what steps still need to be taken. Establishing a timeline for your goals also helps keep you motivated and on track—making sure that nothing slips through the cracks.

When a goal is strategically set, it serves as a powerful tool for guiding progress, allowing us to map out our journey and develop our skills along the way. Goals empower us intrinsically with both insight and structure, enabling us to not only build knowledge but foster confidence in ourselves and all we are capable of achieving. Let's learn how to set and achieve your goals!

When you start something with a set goal in mind, it's natural to be optimistic about the outcome.

You're learning how to surf, and you're confident you'll be standing up and coasting through waves in no time. You start taking painting lessons, and you can't wait to make artwork worth hanging up in your house. Or you bought a bike, and you're already thinking about all the ways you're going to ditch all other modes of transportation.

Beginning a new task with optimism can be really helpful; it's certainly better than going into something thinking you're doomed to fail. But positive thinking can only get you so far. Nobody's perfect, and you're bound to make a few mistakes on the road to achieving your goals—beyond that point, you will need a lot more than beginner's enthusiasm to keep you going.

You're going to spend your whole life learning; it's the foundation for self-improvement. In order to *keep* yourself learning, though, you need a clear and intelligent strategy. You also need to know exactly what you want. Cultivating these wishes and aims will let you see the progress you've made and your future more clearly.

In order to commit yourself to lifelong learning, you need to figure out what you'll be learning in the next year or two. It sounds obvious, but many of us embark on complicated projects of self-improvement without a clear sense of what it is we're actually trying to achieve in the first place. That's why it's important to set goals and to achieve what you set out to do. Even if you don't achieve your goal, or achieve it only partly, you can still feel good about yourself and your abilities, and you'll know exactly what you need to do next to keep striving.

But when you're first beginning to think about what you want to learn, you only think about the good things you'll gain. You're fixated on the outcome, which, although understandable, is precisely what will make you abandon your efforts when you hit that first roadblock. For example, your goal is to lose weight. The thing that inspires you to embark on this goal is fast-forwarding to that glorious moment at the end, when you're feeling light and healthy and proud of yourself. But when the number on the scale is stubbornly refusing to move for the third week in a row, it's hard to tap into those same positive feelings that got you inspired to begin with; instead, you focus on the present negative feelings and tell yourself that dieting makes you miserable and that exercising doesn't work. And you give up on your plan.

The problem wasn't that the scale didn't budge for three weeks—the problem was that you were unprepared to deal with the fact that change takes time. Because your head was filled with all the good feelings of what life would look like *after* your goal was reached, you actually made yourself less resilient to the challenges inherent to the process *before* you met your goal. In other words, your optimism actually worked to sabotage you. The WOOP method can help you get through these tough moments. WOOP relies on the science-backed strategy of mental contrasting, which helps people weigh the benefits and drawbacks of a given plan.

Peer-reviewed studies have shown that the WOOP method can help people reach their goals and change long-ingrained detrimental behaviors. In one experiment, depressed patients who used WOOP, compared to a control method, were significantly more likely to pursue and succeed at their ambitions (Fritzsche et al., 2016). These results are quite common.

So how do you replicate these results for yourself? WOOP stands for wish, outcome, obstacle, and plan. Those who use WOOP set clear goals, visualize outcomes, and then visualize potential setbacks and plan around them. Created by Dr. Gabriele Oettingen of NYU and the University of Hamburg, the method relies on visualization of both aspirations and possible hurdles, as well as the ways you can get out of tough spots.

This means that instead of fixating on the positive successful outcome, you visualize the full process from where you are now to where you want to be. That way, when you encounter (inevitable) obstacles, you are not surprised by them or unprepared to deal with them. You simply encounter any temporary setback as a normal part of the process of change and refuse to let a difficult day derail your entire plan. Once you get the hang of it, it's easy to see why so many find it transformative.

The WOOP method helps you plan for the hard moments. Of course, you should feel confident in yourself when you set off to achieve your goals, and you should get excited about how good life can be once you make the improvements you're dreaming about. But initial confidence that's rooted in "positive thinking" alone will only get you so far. WOOP has been shown to improve performance in activities ranging from physical exercise to academics, and it can improve your life, too (Christiansen et al., 2010).

If you're someone who wants to make your life better or richer in some way, WOOP isn't difficult to practice. All you need to do is take the first step.

Wish: Figuring Out Ambitions and Setting Goals

Ask yourself what you want to achieve. Maybe a lot comes to mind—you want to be a better cook, you want to buy a new computer, you want to learn a new language. All of these are great things to strive for, but you just need to focus on one pursuit for now. There will be plenty of time in your life to master certain skills; it's best just to keep your sights on a single goal at a time.

The first part of the WOOP method is the wish. Let's say you settle on learning a new language. You've always felt that picking up some Spanish would be useful, and you've kind of missed studying something. You like to push yourself, and you know that it's important to keep learning new things throughout your life. You also recognize that foreign languages are pretty valuable.

Learning Spanish will take time, though, especially if you want to become fluent or even just conversational. You need to get *specific* when you're identifying what your wish is. But be careful: If you set the bar too high, you might be setting yourself up for failure. That's because you will be increasing the distance between where you are now and where you want to be—and seeing how big this distance is can be intimidating and overwhelming, causing you to give up. That's not fair to yourself—ambition is great, but you need to be realistic.

Time frames can help, but they're not necessary for the WOOP method to work. You don't need to set an exact deadline. If your wish is to learn Spanish and you're starting from scratch, think about aiming for a set number of words you want to have memorized. Or you could buy a workbook online and push yourself to finish a certain number of pages. You need to make sure that your wish is specific and achievable and that you'll know when you complete it.

"Getting better at Spanish" is not specific enough; there's not really a clear benchmark for knowing that your Spanish has improved. "Memorizing two hundred words in Spanish," meanwhile, is very specific. If you want to accomplish this in a month, you can add in that timeline. You are not keeping your goals modest and achievable because you are not ambitious; instead, you are taking slow and steady steps toward your goal rather than making grand plans and expecting quantum leaps—then getting demoralized when you, of course, don't reach that goal overnight.

Once you have a sure wish—one that you'll be able to recognize when it's achieved—then you'll know exactly what to do.

Outcome: Understanding What's to Come

You did it! You learned the two hundred words that you said you wanted to learn. You made flashcards, you practiced regularly, and now when you walk down the street, you can see that the stop sign is *rojo*, and the *coches* on the road are going way too fast.

Try to imagine that moment. The next step in the WOOP method is the outcome, which relies on a lot of visualization. You have to be able to fast forward in time and see yourself having achieved your goal. Think about what your life will be like when you've done what you set out to do. What would the best outcome be? How do you think you'll feel?

Visualizing your outcome enables you to understand better *why* it is you want to fulfill this particular wish. Specificity is super important in this step, too. You won't be nearly as excited to follow through with your plans if you only have a vague idea of what that accomplishment will feel like or how your life will improve. When you can really see how something will make your life better, the prospect of learning about a new topic or learning how to do a new task will make you feel much more motivated.

If somebody really wants to learn how to knit, a good goal for them would be to knit a certain item—even something pretty simple, like a scarf. That person could then think about making a cozy scarf for themselves, wearing it out in winter, feeling immensely proud for learning how to create clothing instead of just going to the store for something new.

They'll have mastered a pattern to make an article of clothing, which requires a lot of hours spent making stitches work together. It's more of an undertaking than some people realize, and it might not always go well.

But, as we've already seen, this part of the WOOP framework may be relatively easy, and you may have already thoroughly imagined the end result.

In that case, it's important to visualize the drawbacks of this outcome, too; their hands might feel kind of cramped after all that work, or they find that the scarf they knitted really isn't as attractive as something they could find on the rack at a department store. They might finish the project and feel good about having completed one article of clothing, but they might not feel comfortable out and about, wearing a scarf with some lumps and flaws.

Similarly, you might want to consider the way you're thinking about the outcome. Perhaps you make the scarf and feel immensely proud of your creative efforts, but discover in real life that wearing the thing actually brings you little joy. You thought it would be great to walk around in this scarf, but somehow when you were done, real life didn't quite feel like how you imagined. Has this ever happened to you? It's usually because you didn't pay enough close attention to *how* you visualized the outcome. You need to honestly ask why a goal appeals to you, and what you're imagining you will achieve from it. Does the scarf goal represent mastery at a craft? Or is it that you want others to compliment your unique style? Or do you like the idea of being sustainable and not buying fast fashion? Try to clearly understand your psychological motivations.

Memorizing a set number of words in Spanish might feel great for a while, but you might start to feel like you still have so far to go before you really begin to understand the language. You'll have to keep learning many more words and grammar rules. Becoming at least conversational in Spanish would mean being able to talk to Spanish speakers with relative ease and understand Spanish-language music and movies. So, in this case, the goal is a necessary one, but it's not sufficient. You need to keep going.

Imagining the different elements of your outcome—both benefits and drawbacks—helps to make the visualization richer. And the richer your visualization, the more control and mastery you have over its manifestation in reality. The WOOP method succeeds because participants engage in this mental contrasting, comparing good and bad aspects of an outcome. Achievement of your goal won't make everything in your life perfect, and the path to said goal won't be clear of stumbles, either. But the irony is that the more clearly you can understand and delineate this, the more likely you are to actually achieve your outcome and be satisfied with it.

Obstacle: Running into Problems and Visualizing Hurdles

This is arguably the most important part of the framework since it's something most of us never think to do. Consider all the potential obstacles to your plan and what you will do to prepare to overcome them. You'll be visualizing in this step, too; the WOOP method emphasizes this and has been shown to reduce feelings of disappointment and regret because of this contrast of expectations (Krott et al., 2018). You need to understand how the hard work of this task will feel before you are facing it in real life.

What's keeping you from getting what you want? Is it the enormity of the goal or is it really your feelings of being intimidated by the goal? We need optimism but also to realize that achieving any ambition won't be an easy task. This is important: The task WILL be difficult. Sometimes the sheer recognition of this fact can be an insurmountable obstacle for people who set out to accomplish something.

Maybe your obstacles are internal. Perhaps you've never been very good at languages in the past, so while you want to study Spanish, you feel like it won't come naturally to you. It's just not something you have an aptitude for. Or perhaps you do have some skill in learning languages, but you have a lot of difficulty with time management. The idea of regularly setting aside time to memorize a bunch of words feels overwhelming. You struggle with your schedule enough as is!

And there can be external obstacles to your plans, too. You're not great with managing your time, and you also just don't have a lot of free time, between work and chores and family life. You think that taking classes would be ideal—you'd have an obligation to show up, given that you have to get your money's worth—but it's too expensive for you at the moment.

But whatever your obstacles are, they will also be more destructive if you are unaware of them and do nothing to anticipate and prepare for them. If you are trying to lose weight, you might fail to take into account the fact that your office goes out for lunch every Friday, and they tend to eat extremely tempting junk food. If you simply forget about this obstacle, by the time Friday rolls around and you're handed a menu, your plan is already derailed. You binge on loads of junk food, and your goal is over before it starts. But if you had taken the time to carefully visualize everything that could possibly stand in your way, you would have seen the Friday lunchtime temptation from a mile away and would have made a plan on Thursday to avoid it. Then, you would have stayed on track.

If you don't grasp that things won't always go the way you planned, you'll be much more likely to quit when trouble actually emerges. This is the central problem with positive thinking—everything can be rosy and blissful in your imagination, but real life inevitably intervenes. How will you cope with that? Truthfully, the answer is that many of us give up in frustration! In the heat of the moment, your rosy goal evaporates into nothing, and the double cheeseburger with fries and the chocolate cake for dessert suddenly seem like a much better idea.

The WOOP method helps you encounter struggles head-on, and with conscious awareness so you're much more likely to succeed in your goals.

Plan: Finding Strategies to Overcome Errors

So you know now that everything's not going to go swimmingly. If this all seems aimed to make you throw in the towel early, don't worry. Everything takes effort; that's what the WOOP method emphasizes. You're going to be learning and working on yourself for the rest of your life. It's important to recognize that it's not going to be easy all the time. The sooner you acknowledge this, the sooner you can work around it—and that's empowering.

The final step of the WOOP method teaches you to come up with a plan. Specifically, you should frame this as an "if-then plan." If something gets in your way, then you'll figure out how to overcome it. Sometimes, it's valuable to simply be aware of the fact that struggling is not actually a problem. How many of us are completely confused and enraged when things don't go according to plan? But struggling with a project is not a sign that something is wrong—in fact, it's a sign that we're growing, learning, and changing!

You've already visualized what will happen to you if you meet your goal. And you've visualized potential hurdles coming from both yourself and the world at large. If you're still determined to succeed—and you should be!—then you now have to imagine what you'll do if things do start to go south.

If you're trying to study Spanish and you find that you don't think you have enough time to put in the work needed to memorize your vocabulary, what will you do? Only picturing the happiness you'll feel when you learn the words you wanted to learn could make you give up when you realize that it actually takes effort to succeed. But with the WOOP method, you'll have prepared for this scenario. You already know that you're not great at managing your time. Ask yourself: "If I find that I'm not organizing my time well to study, what will I do?"

You could find ways to squeeze Spanish study into unoccupied parts of your day. Maybe you could listen to some audio review on your commute home from work. Instead of scrolling through your phone when you first wake up, find an app that lets you make flash cards, and review those. Look for a partner who will practice with you, someone you know will stick to a schedule.

Once you've figured out your tactic, clearly articulate your if-then plan. If you find yourself running out of time to practice Spanish, then you'll look through vocab words on your phone first thing in the morning. If you feel like you can't manage your time at all, then find a friend to practice with you. If you're struggling to find time to study a text, then you can look for podcasts or other audio resources. If you can't quite motivate yourself, then give yourself some small rewards after a task.

Make sure that the plan will fit into your lifestyle—if you're not someone who checks their phone first thing in the morning, the former example probably won't suit you. You have to look for foolproof ways that you know will lead to success.

These contingency plans will really help you meet the expectations you set for yourself. As with previous steps, visualization is key. Imagine implementing the plan you're making for yourself. What will it feel like to wake up every day and practice this new skill? Will you go through the day much more relaxed, knowing that you've already accomplished a task you'd been struggling with?

You can even write your plan down in the if-then style if you think that this could help you later on. At the very least, repeat it a few times to drill it home: "If I'm not organizing my time well enough to study Spanish, I'll look at my flash cards right when I wake up."

Use your own wish and potential obstacle to fill in the formula, of course. You'll find that going in with this type of preparation will make you feel much more confident at the start of your practice. And when you do start to slip, you'll know what to do.

Chapter Takeaways

- WOOP (Wish, Outcome, Obstacle, and Plan) is an evidence-based intervention that guides you through an investigation of hurdles and barriers while introducing you to goal-setting. This evidence-based approach is great because it allows individuals to create a plan that addresses any difficulties they may face while also considering their desired outcome. Practicing the WOOP method helps to build confidence, increase motivation, and foster a sense of self-efficacy, which can be beneficial when striving to attain personal goals.

- First, identify your wish or goal in detail, being clear about how you know when you've achieved it. Consider something in your life that you wish to improve: your career, education, relationships, or anything else. It should be challenging, realistic, and achievable.

- Next, flesh out this outcome in your mind's eye, visualizing both the good and bad aspects. Visualizing your outcome helps you understand why you want to accomplish this specific goal. Specificity here is important because you won't be nearly as motivated to carry out your ideas if you have a hazy sense of what success would feel like or how your life would improve.

- Carefully consider the obstacles in this plan, being honest and realistic about the unavoidable effort and challenge involved. Consider what it might look and feel like to have your objective met. Spend some time thoroughly imagining, seeing, and feeling what it would be like to achieve the finest potential outcome.

- Finally, make a plan that addresses these obstacles so you'll know what to do when setbacks occur. This is important because keeping your options open will help you get up when things don't go your way.

CHAPTER FOUR: Self-Education Begins and Ends with Questions

It's all too easy to take what we've been taught at face value, never really questioning our understanding and getting hung up on the details. Learning how to critically question our own thinking and understanding can open doors that turn tedious information into untapped potential. When we learn how to learn for ourselves, it not only keeps our intrinsic motivation alive by unearthing knowledge rather than waiting for someone else to spoon-feed it, but it also helps us find gratification in everything from small victories to larger solutions that offer insights into what truly means something to us—our passions!

Taking a step back every once in a while and asking ourselves "Why am I doing this?" and "How can I be better at this?" can be an invaluable tool when growing into our greatest selves. Let's look at how we can improve our learning strategies and *learn* how to learn.

Kai was a bright and talented student, but he had always found it hard to focus. He would drift off during classes, struggle to stay motivated when given an assignment, and never quite get the grades he knew he was capable of. His teachers were supportive, but they couldn't seem to help him break through his own mental blocks. Kai never asked questions in class even if he knew he needed the clarification. When Kai's parents noticed how frustrated he was becoming with himself, they decided it was time for a change. They enrolled him in a special program that promised to teach students how to become better learners by developing their self-awareness and sharpening their critical thinking skills.

At first, Kai wasn't sure if this program could really make any difference in his academic performance; after all, how did asking himself questions have anything to do with getting good grades? And it was fine that he didn't pose any questions in class; he could just go home and reread the chapter or something. It all seemed very pointless.

But as the weeks went on and Kai began putting into practice the lessons from the program, such as learning how to ask yourself and others questions about topics like: "Why am I having trouble understanding this concept?" "What strategies can I use here?" "How can I remember this information more effectively?" "Can you please elaborate on this with an example?" Something began changing inside of him.

He slowly developed greater insight into why certain things felt so difficult for him before; now armed with new tools at his disposal that allowed him to explore these issues from different perspectives, progress came much easier than ever before. As each day passed, Kai felt his confidence grow stronger and stronger until eventually there no longer seemed any obstacle too daunting or a problem too complex for him to tackle head-on!

Kai is now thriving in school thanks largely to being able to develop powerful self-questioning habits for effective self-education. The habits enable him to confront every challenge with newfound enthusiasm, find out answers to his questions, and communicate with his teachers more effectively, thus proving once again just how important asking the right questions is in taking control of your own journey toward lifelong learning.

A study revealed that self-questioning procedures greatly increased lecture comprehension over time. The findings implied that practicing a self-questioning, information-processing approach can significantly increase college students' understanding of lectures (King, 1989). So many of us, like Kai, are so afraid to ask important questions due to fear of sounding silly or stupid.

Asking the right questions to others and most importantly yourself can be the key to personal and/or professional growth. It can help diversify our own thoughts as we enlist the help of other people in helping us answer our most important queries. When you ask questions, you add to your knowledge, and that alone is the most effective kind of learning there is.

By getting an honest look at where we stand, we can make informed decisions that will set us up for success in any given area of life. Questions give us direction, help us identify changes that need to be made, and push us to explore new possibilities. They encourage us to evaluate what we've been doing so far and open our eyes to potential paths that were not previously available and serve as an invaluable tool for anyone looking to broaden their horizons and rise above current situations or limitations. The best thing about it? It's free! All it takes is a genuine desire for development and you're off!

Your success depends on more than just hard work. Therefore, it's critical to ask the right questions. If you don't ask enough questions or the right ones, your chances of succeeding in whatever endeavor you choose plummet. For example, you are a hardworking student who dreams of going to college. You work tirelessly for years, balancing two part-time jobs and attending high school classes in the hopes of one day achieving this goal. But it seems like an impossible dream. That is, until you hear about the scholarship program at your local school. You get excited, begin the application process, but receive a rejection letter two months later. Dejected, you ask yourself, "Why didn't I get this scholarship? What could I have done to make my application stronger?"

Do you notice a difference? The second question is empowering and one that will lead you to success. Of course, you must be persistent and motivated in order to find a solution. However, simply asking yourself the right question will dramatically increase your odds of succeeding if you focus on what you can improve rather than focusing on the why-nots and the what-ifs.

Now that we have established how important mastering the art of questioning is for effective self-learning, it's time to get into exactly how you can do that.

How to Use Questions to Pull Information From Anywhere

The immense, uncharted area of human experience that exists outside the restrictive bounds of formal schooling is the most significant frontier of education. The vast majority of people do not attend educational institutions. Even the most well-educated persons have five decades or more to live after graduation. Yet, the need for learning does not disappear. The desire to improve, to continuously learn, does not cease to exist. It just becomes more and more urgent as you get older. Begin by asking yourself, "How can this requirement be met?" "How can the learning potential of this massive and rapidly rising non-school population be realized?" Especially since when you are out of school, you then have an opportunity to learn whatever your heart desires, and this is the stage where effective lifelong learning begins.

Cal Newport's book *Deep Work: Rules for Focused Success in a Distracted World* demonstrates that the only way to advance in today's economy is to learn difficult but relevant things rapidly. Not very good news for my anxiety-laden heart, but I guess it's worth a try, yes? Take a deep breath and let's begin! (This is more for me than for you).

Start by asking yourself the right question relevant to your unique situation. Make sure that the questions you are asking are empowering (e.g., "What strategy can I adopt to improve my CGPA?" instead of "Why did I fail two classes this semester?"). Notice how the first one actually prompts you to do better and improve. Empowering questions are solution-oriented and will usually begin with "how." For example, "How can I make this situation better?" "How do I reach my goal this year?" "How can I improve my posture?" "How can I improve my relationships?"

Avoid all disempowering questions, specifically ones that focus on the "whys" of a situation. They are victimizing and focus on regret, loss, and frustration. Focusing on just the negative aspects can make you overlook any possibility of a solution. Following are some examples of the kind of questions you should definitely be avoiding: "Why did I fail this semester?" "Why is everyone else doing so much better than I am?" "Why am I so unlucky?"

Now that you have mastered the art of asking the right questions, it's time to ask the right people. You don't want to just go up to a random person and demand they answer your questions. So how do we locate the right people? Let's say that you are in the midst of learning how to be a photographer. You are not going to go up to a painter and ask them, "How do I set up my own photography studio?" They're obviously not going to be able to help you as much as an actual photographer would.

Therefore, seek out those who have already achieved what you hope to master and use them as your role models. Ponder and ask them what it was that made them such a success. Reach out in person or pick up a book that they wrote on the topic; either way, by getting insight from seasoned professionals, effective lifelong learning will be much easier.

Find mentors and enjoy watching knowledge grow at lightning speed! Prior to asking the right person, decide what you want to get out of this interaction. What do you hope to discover? What do you hope to do using that information? Then look for others who have already accomplished that.

Now that you have the right person, it's time to ask them the right questions. Asking open-ended questions is an invaluable skill. Not only do they allow us to get to the heart of a given problem or situation, but they are also great icebreakers that can help people feel more comfortable opening up and sharing information with us. Avoid making general inquiries or asking for yes/no answers; instead, strive for questions that begin with words like "how" and "what," which will make your conversation partner more likely to provide a longer and more reflective answer.

Some open-ended questions are:

- "How did you achieve that scholarship?"
- "What are the most important strategies you'd recommend for me?"
- "What documents will I be needing?"

Make sure you specify your questions as the conversation flows. For example, "What was the one thing you think played the most significant part in helping you achieve that scholarship?"

Also consider what kind of language you're using: Leading questions rarely yield fruitful dialogue, as anyone can easily sense when someone is taking them in a certain direction. For best results with any kind of conversation going forward, remember to listen just as much as you speak; listening attentively provides richer opportunities for follow-up and further exploration into whatever topics are at hand.

Practicing active listening is one of the best things you can do to help improve communication with others. It involves actively understanding what somebody is saying by paying attention to the words they are saying, their body language, and underlying emotions so that you can better understand their point of view. To practice active listening, start by making sure you are in a quiet space and giving the speaker your full attention. Do not interrupt while they are talking.

As they talk, listen closely and paraphrase what they're telling you back to them in order to ensure understanding on both sides. Not only will this help to settle any misunderstandings but also show that you have given real thought about what was said, which is often appreciated. Lastly, don't be afraid to give your own thoughts or ask more open-ended questions if there's something that isn't clear; just make sure it's done politely and respectfully!

You can practice by spicing up a conversation with your besties or partner by dedicating ten minutes to homing in on the power of listening. Use this time as an opportunity to ask engaging questions that let them share stories and experiences, while avoiding any interruptions! Once they are done, you can dive even deeper into their thoughts and feelings.

Concentrate on the solution. Whenever you pose any kind of question, always think about the solution. This applies to both self-questioning and asking other people. Your subconscious will immediately draw your attention toward whatever you are focusing on. For example, if as a photographer all you're focusing on is how saturated the market is or how nobody is going to appreciate your style or hire you... well, then that is always where you're going to end up!

You'll always find solutions for any difficulty or issue if you concentrate on finding solutions and view challenges as chances to learn more. Therefore, being solution-focused and concentrating on the opportunities rather than the risks are the key components of asking the right questions and pave the way for lifelong learning to take place unhindered.

Bloom's Taxonomy: A Method You Can Use for Effective Self-Questioning

Critical thinking is so important to acknowledge, especially as we navigate through various scenarios in life. From complex work tasks requiring finesse and attention to detail, to helping our children with their school assignments, to tackling daily issues, having the ability to think critically can be a great asset.

To foster this important skill, Bloom's taxonomy offers an accessible framework to define and classify the various levels of human cognition (thinking, learning, and comprehending). This taxonomy divides cognition into six distinct levels, from one being the most basic up until six that requires more in-depth thought processing. When self-learning, it is important to know how to self-question based on the following six categories.

Remembering Knowledge

This stage concentrates on retrieving information from memory that has been obtained through instruction and experience. During this process, the learner must be able to recognize or recall relevant learned material such as facts or terms with accuracy and fluency.

This could be done by using mnemonics, repetition, images, and other memorization techniques. Retaining previously learned knowledge helps provide a foundation for higher levels of critical thinking and problem-solving skills as they move up Bloom's taxonomy. Some questions that you can ask yourself to keep the momentum of knowledge going are:

- What can I recall about_____?
- How would I define_____?
- Can I identify_____?
- Can I compare and contrast_____?
- Describe the process of_____?
- What would I choose_____?

Insert anything that you are currently thinking about mastering. This is about you remembering important information, such as the definition of a word. For example, what can I recall about thermodynamics? How would I define thermodynamics? Can I identify the laws of thermodynamics? These kinds of questions can help you identify what information you know and what you need to know.

Understanding

The second stage of knowledge in Bloom's taxonomy is all about understanding the material rather than just memorizing it. To reach this level, you'll need to go beyond studying; great comprehension requires engaging with the material.

That may mean discussing ideas within the material with others, analyzing and evaluating different arguments made in the material, or forming connections between that material and other related topics. It's an excellent way to really get beneath the surface of what you're learning and can help ensure greater levels of mastery.

Questions you can ask yourself:

- What can I infer from_____?
- What did I observe_____?
- How would I identify_____?
- Can I elaborate on_____?

For example, what can I infer from the summary I wrote of *Jane Eyre*'s first chapter? What did I observe in the teacher's note that was contrary to what I had mentioned? How would I identify these themes within the text? Can I elaborate on the theme of feminism? These are the kinds of questions you need to be asking yourself as you move on from remembering to understanding.

Application

The third stage of application in Bloom's taxonomy is all about taking the information we've learned and being able to use it in a practical sense. This could involve putting pieces of information together or adapting them for different purposes, as well as applying different theories and ideas.

Activities such as solving math problems, creating detailed essays and plans, discovering patterns, or designing experiments are all common examples of activities that involve the third level of application. Overall, this stage emphasizes both learning content and understanding how to use it outside of traditional lecture settings. In doing so, you will gain valuable knowledge that you can carry over into your everyday life.

Questions you can ask yourself:

- How would I alter_____to_____?
- What examples can I find that _____?
- How would I solve_____?

Ask yourself, how would I alter the excerpt I have already written on the major themes in *Jane Eyre* so that it includes more of my own opinion than anybody else's? Can I write a detailed commentary on Chapter 5? What examples can I find that will support my own interpretation of it?" All very practical questions to help you apply the concepts you have learned in a better way.

Analyzing

The fourth stage of application in Bloom's taxonomy is all about taking the knowledge gained from prior stages surrounding remembering, understanding, and analyzing, and using it to create something that's entirely original.

Rather than just remembering the facts or understanding why something has happened, this stage requires people to actually use these pieces of information, whether it be writing a story or designing an experiment for learning objectives like problem-solving and critical thinking. It's an interactive and adaptive process that puts the entirety of Bloom's taxonomy into practice.

Questions to ask yourself:

- How would I explain_____?
- What can I point out about_____?
- What is the problem with_____?
- Which of my ideas validate_____?

For example, how would I explain how so far ahead of its time *Jane Eyre* is? What text can I point out in regard to the themes I am looking for? Which of my ideas validate the concepts I drafted in my essay earlier?

Evaluating

The fifth stage of application in this theoretical structure is evaluation. Evaluation involves assessing the value or success of something by collecting information and analyzing it against predetermined standards. One way to incorporate evaluation into learning activities is through problem-based instruction.

This type of activity asks individuals to consider a problem or case study from multiple perspectives with their own opinions before giving a conclusion or solution. By actively engaging in thoughtful discussion, critically analyzing information, and making informed decisions about various topics, you can develop important skills that enable you to become a more independent thinker.

Questions to ask yourself:

- What is my opinion of_____?
- How could I verify_____?
- What information would I use to prioritize_____?

For instance, what is my opinion of how women were treated back in the day? Where do I stand on equal rights for both men and women? How could I verify some of this book's historical background that I dug up? What information should I prioritize? My own ramblings or those of my professor? Both?

Creating

The sixth stage in Bloom's taxonomy is an important step for higher-level learning; it requires synthesizing and creating. Examples of this include taking ideas from multiple sources and integrating them together to form something new. This could involve analyzing a process and then creating a new solution, creating a presentation that illustrates understanding of material, designing a new product, or writing a manual. The synthesis and creation stages help you think critically and make logical connections among ideas in order to draw applicable conclusions.

Questions to ask yourself:

- How would I compile the facts for_____?
- How would I elaborate on the reason_____?
- How would I improve_____?
- What could I invent_____?
- What facts can I gather_____?
- Can I predict the outcome if_____?

For example, how would I compile all the facts for my essay? For my thesis? For my presentation? How would I elaborate on the theme of feminism in *Jane Eyre*? How would I improve my paper by connecting to the other themes in the book? Can I predict the outcome of my paper if I just go with my instinct and not really listen to anyone else's opinion? All of these questions are going to help you in creating something really new and exciting.

The CAFE Framework: Compression, Frequency, and Encoding

Donald Maudsley used the word "meta-learning" to refer to the process by which people start to influence what they learn, taking more and more "**control of habits of perception, exploration, learning, and growth that they have internalized**." Later, psychologists and cognitive scientists would refer to meta-learning as "learning how to learn." Meta-learning strategies like the DiSSS (Deconstruction, Selection, Sequencing, Stakes) and CaFE (compression, frequency, and encoding) frameworks by Tim Ferriss can help us in honing our study skills and problem-solving strategies. They can assist us in rapidly teaching ourselves a plethora of new topics in a short amount of time and achieving a level of competency in a wide range of areas of interest.

I will be focusing on the CaFE framework, as it is significantly more applicable and actionable. However, before we get into the intricacies of the CaFE framework, let's take a quick look at why meta-learning is so powerful.

One example of meta-learning in action is musical instruction: By placing emphasis on understanding music theory and improving listening comprehension, musicians can ultimately use these concepts to develop complex improvisational skills. Other domains where meta-learning benefits individuals include language acquisition, task management and organizational skills, academic study habits for both college and professional degrees, sports training, and more.

Unlike traditional methods of instruction that grant us a one-off success, masterful meta-learners who make good use of meta-learning strategies understand that good results come from continual lifelong practice; they continue to invest time into self-education and refine the ways they use and make sense of their knowledge. Think about the last time you learned something new. Was the most recent item you learned from a class you took five years ago or in high school?

Of course not; as humans, we are continuously learning new concepts and abilities and changing our worldviews. We don't need to be in school or at a conference to learn something new; because of the power of the internet, we have several lifetimes' worth of knowledge in the palm of our hand, ready to be learned. In school, we not only learn algebra, geometry, and physics, but we also learn how to learn. So, how does meta-learning help us become better lifelong learners?

Each time you actively learn something new, the neurons in your brain wire together to form new neural circuits. The connections that define these neural circuits become stronger as you learn more (Dehaene, 2020), implying that learning is a positive feedback loop: The more effectively you learn now, the easier it becomes to learn in the future. So, what does this have to do with lifelong learning? As previously stated, the more we learn now, the easier it will be to learn in the future. Lifelong learning is an invaluable habit to adopt and can benefit every aspect of your life.

With more knowledge and skills to draw upon, not only will you be better equipped to tackle difficult tasks, but you'll also have a greater appreciation for the world around you. Learning new things often brings joy and excitement as well; with an open attitude toward continued learning, you'll never have to worry about feeling bored or stagnant! Making a habit of lifelong learning will give you the boost to reach success, both personal and professional, throughout your lifetime.

Meta-learning frameworks like the CaFE method give you the time to reflect and help you build an understanding of your own learning style and apply different strategies toward it. Instead of just following instructions and doing it "right," you can take a step back, think, and question what you are doing in order to experience the process itself.

During psychological group interventions, I often hear phrases like: "I gave myself time to stop and think," "I used my imagination to take charge," or even "I concentrate hard and believe in myself." This kind of thinking allows you to go beyond simply ticking off tasks and to learn how to take ownership over your learning journeys. Meta-processes provide valuable insight that wouldn't be possible without giving thought to the process behind the activity at hand, allowing you to explore your potential in deeper ways (Watkins, 2000, 2005, 2015).

Now that we have established how important meta-learning strategies can be, it's time to unravel the intricacies of the CaFE framework.

How to Approach Learning Something New: The CaFE Framework

Everyone has a passion for something, whether it be writing, web design, or cooking. The challenge is to take that passion and turn it into a highly coveted skill. Do you want to study art? Okay, but it's possible that after spending a lot of money on art books and supplies and being enthusiastic about playing it, you end up shoving everything under your bed and forgetting about it after a few weeks. How do we fight this? How do we not let the enormous amount of information available out there overwhelm us? **Tim employs "compression" in the CaFE approach to simplify the essentials of his objective to a few bare-bones notes.** He advises that we start by condensing the most essential 20 percent (selected through a careful deliberation process) into a cheat sheet.

As a university student, I initially assumed that the most effective tool for preparing for my midterms and final examinations would be my laptop or my phone. I had no idea my best companion before exams would be a blank piece of paper, highlighters, and a pen. A piece of paper that, once filled out, I would guard with my life. As a result, my adventure with cheat sheets commenced, complete with errors, victories, and lessons learned.

When it pertains to cheat sheets, there is a lot of variety. There are several font sizes, text-image ratios, colors, and column counts. Although a cheat sheet is intended to correspond with your personal learning preferences, there are a few tips that apply to everyone, regardless of what you are trying to master. Begin by using a blank sheet of paper, a pencil, an eraser, some colorful markers, and your favorite stickers to make it super fancy!

Make a line across the top of the sheet and fill in your contact information. Draw columns along both sides of the sheet. Select your color scheme. When it comes to creating a "beautiful" cheat sheet, having a decent color code makes all the difference. I frequently use the same color code, which allows me to avoid mistakes and always have sheets with a very clear color code that is error-free. It's not only a matter of aesthetics; it also makes it easier to discover information quickly. Because the written content is so small, a good color code is essential if you want to locate relevant information quickly.

I take my preferred colors and write the subject, subtitle, example, and definition, and I frequently use green for the advantages and red for the disadvantages on a page next to me. In literature, for example, I also use a specific color to highlight themes and key terms. That makes it easier for me to locate them when necessary. You can also employ bold fonts throughout the sheet to make locating sections easier.

The second step we have within the CaFe framework is frequency. Consider asking yourself, how frequently should I practice? What are my constraints or objectives? When it comes to planning any sort of study schedule for rapid skill acquisition, it's important to take into account your goals and your personal limits. Consider the amount of time you have available each day, plus when any upcoming deadlines or exams might be, so that you don't find yourself in a stressful situation without enough preparation.

Begin by incorporating learning into your calendar; finding time is critical for good learning, but it is also tough because time is a limited resource, even when it comes to online learning, which has typically taken less time than on-site learning. There is a variety of viewpoints on how and what you should include in your learning plans in order to keep yourself motivated and obtain the highest results and success rate possible. So how can you create a schedule for learning that works?

To create your personal learning schedule, consider four factors: study duration, time of day, weekday, and frequency. A few conditions influence the appropriate length of a learning session. The first is your own ability to focus (Lamba, 2014). This could be one hour for some, thirty minutes for others, but longer times are also feasible. If you're not sure what duration is best for you, just experiment. Choose a different duration for each learning session and discover your own preferences! Your work calendar is another aspect that influences your learning time. If your schedule is already full and only a few occasions remain, it may make sense to choose shorter periods.

For me, acknowledging my own limits is critical for staying productive and making progress. In other words, I need to know how much time I can sit down and really focus on learning before I start to burn out. It's different for everybody, but for me, it usually works out to around three to four hours of deep work a day with breaks in between, depending on the situation. That's why it's important to realistically evaluate how often and for how long you should study in order to make meaningful progress without putting too much pressure on yourself.

According to recent research (Kaur 2021), learners who study in the morning perform better than those who study in the late afternoon or evening, with the afternoon representing the most unproductive hour of the day. Still, we can all agree on one thing: Some people simply thrive in the morning, while others can focus better in the afternoon or evening, and this is unlikely to change! To be successful, it is critical to devote part of your quality cognitive time to learning. You wouldn't want to spend your quality cognitive time partying, only to focus on learning when you're tired and spent out.

It is critical to continue studying throughout one's life in order to have a lifelong learning experience. According to studies, the early weeks are frequently the most active, before time investment falls relatively quickly (Yeomans, 2010). A regular learning schedule on your calendar will help you avoid this. With it, you can select your preferred study time, location, and duration.

When helping my clients learn different mindfulness techniques, they often ask, "How often should I practice?" To learn well, you need a combination of spaced practice, cramming, interspersed practice, and regular testing. So, for example, when it comes to baking, I attempt to cook simply on weeknights by studying techniques, ingredient usage, and flavor pairings. I frequently challenge myself with brief baking marathons and an ambitious menu when I entertain (cramming). These brief sprints allow for a lot of learning in a short period of time. It is also a good way to get rapid input from others. If you're prepared, cramming can be useful.

There's also spaced and interleaved practice. For example, I'll enroll in a class on a particular method and then practice it at home a month or so later (and on a regular basis after that) to ensure I don't forget, putting it into a recipe. Even if you're acquiring a lifelong skill, setting deadlines for phases of learning is quite beneficial. Learning on the fly is neither efficient nor cost-effective. When you select your deadline, utilize deconstruction and other approaches mentioned here to prepare resources, learning stages, and your scheduled calendar; set a goal for the conclusion of each level of learning.

Coding is the last component of Tim's rapid skill acquisition toolset. This requires you to connect new information to prior knowledge, making use of the associative nature of memory. One illustration of this is the acronym CaFE. By compressing and tying the framework to the already-ingrained phrase cafe, we strengthen the new information's hold on the mind. There are numerous encoding techniques (using acronyms or mnemonic devices, for example). Declarative knowledge can be remembered very well using this method. Encoding can be used to practice other subjects you are learning. Tim Ferriss, for instance, took Japanese calligraphy classes in addition to his Japanese language studies.

Crafting an acronym can be fun, especially when you're trying to be creative. It involves selecting a phrase or sentence and coming up with words to take the first letter of each one to create the acronym. To make it easier, start off by writing a phrase that's easy to remember and relevant to what you want it to represent. Then look for single words (or syllables) so it reads better in shorthand. For example, "NASA" stands for National Aeronautics and Space Administration, while "AIDS" is acquired immunodeficiency syndrome. With a little brainstorming and imagination, you, too, can create your own memorable acronym!

Mnemonic techniques are another widely used encoding technique. These are tools to aid memory that enable us to connect new information to previously learned material. Imagery is one of the most used mnemonic techniques. It has been used for thousands of years to help people recall information by using visuals. The fascinating thing about imagery is that the better the encoding, the weirder the image. Imagine that you are attempting to remember that the mitochondria is the cell's main source of energy. You may visualize a dust mite flexing its muscles to help you remember this (you gotta admit, it kinda does look like that). I am aware that it is odd and slightly repulsive. But it's pictures like this that will improve and fortify relationships to aid lifelong learning.

Singing a song or remembering a rhyme is an awesome way to learn something new, like the many educational and fun kids' songs parents teach their kids. Just about everyone remembers the nursery rhymes learned in childhood, "Hey Diddle Diddle" and "Twinkle, Twinkle, Little Star," for example. Then there is the planet song from kindergarten (do you know the planets in the solar system? lalalala), and I bet most of us still recall the ABC song for learning our ABCs.

Simple tunes repeat words often enough to cement them into our memories and make it easy to call them up again when necessary. Others use jingles with a catchy melody and rhythm to help remember words better than if they'd just been read out of context. Whatever method you decide on, it's worth giving it a try; injecting some music or rhythm into remembering can truly do the trick!

Coming up with funny sentences to remember the spelling or order of something may seem trivial at first, but you'll be glad you took the time when you find yourself in the middle of a situation where accuracy is key. Inventing silly sayings can be a clever way to store information in your head and make it easier to recall later on down the line. (For example, memorizing the sentence "flowered unicorns came happily singing in awe" to remember the spelling of the word fuchsia.

Some think outside-of-the-box solutions like this might just become your secret weapon for conquering anxiety and helping to improve your memorization skills. Making up creative ideas such as this could prove very helpful and could open up lots of new mental pathways for storing data over time.

Chapter Takeaways

- It is important to ask the right questions when learning something new, especially if you want to learn it effectively. Empowering questions that are solution-oriented and begin with "how" will help you get started on the right foot. You should also avoid disempowering questions that focus on the negative aspects of a situation and begin with "why."
- Bloom's taxonomy offers a framework to define and classify the levels of human cognition, from basic to more in-depth thought processing. With self-learning, it is important to know how to self-question based on the following six categories: remembering, understanding, applying, analyzing, evaluating, and creating.

- Remembering knowledge: This stage concentrates on retrieving information from memory that has been obtained through instruction and experience. To do this effectively, try using mnemonics or other memorization techniques.
- Understanding: The second stage of knowledge is all about understanding the material rather than just memorizing it. Try discussing ideas within the material with others or forming connections between that material and related topics.
- Application: The third stage of application is about taking what you have learned and being able to use it in a practical sense outside of lecture settings, such as solving math problems or creating detailed essays/plans.
- Analyzing: The fourth stage of analysis consists of taking the knowledge gained from prior stages and using it to create something original, like writing a story or designing an experiment.
- Everyone has a passion for something, but it is a challenge to take that passion and turn it into a highly coveted skill. To fight this, CaFE suggests compressing the most essential 20 percent of information into a cheat sheet. Consider four factors when creating your personal learning schedule: study duration, time of day, weekday, and frequency. Encoding is the last component of Tim's rapid skill acquisition toolset and requires you to connect new information to prior knowledge.

CHAPTER FIVE: The Sacred, Life-Changing Habit of Reading

It's no secret that reading has been touted as the key to unlocking a world of knowledge and expanding your intellectual capacity. By building a habit of daily reading, you can stay informed on current events, learn more about a particular subject, or maybe even get intrinsically motivated to reach those big goals. Doing so also helps open your mind to new ideas, prepares you for unfamiliar scenarios, and gives you the skills to succeed in almost any situation.

It's no wonder many successful people cite reading as one of the best ways to achieve success and become smarter. So, if you're looking for a way to accelerate your learning experience and reach your goals faster, then making a habit of daily reading is definitely worth considering!

Ask any permanent student of life or successful autodidact what their most consistent habit is and you may find they give the same answer: reading.

Reading is something that we all know is good for us, but it's also something that we often have mountains of excuses for not doing. You've probably had at least one of these excuses when it comes to not reading more: *I just don't have the time! I don't have the patience!* And perhaps the most common—*I just don't know where to start!*

Those are all valid excuses, but the key to becoming an effective daily reader is in your hands. Once you learn to employ some of the methods experts advocate to become a daily reader, you'll find that reading opens up a whole new world for you, making you a better person in the process.

You'll find that your mind is stimulated and your curiosity about the world is piqued. Perhaps most important, becoming a daily reader will help you appreciate both sides of every argument and be more critical of "facts" you already know . . . or think you know. And in today's world, where everyone seems to have the "my way or the highway" philosophy, looking at things from all sides is a skill in short supply.

How do we squeeze more reading into our lives?

Take Advantage of Free Time

There's no doubt we live in a fast-paced hustle-and-bustle world. Family commitments and careers take up most of our time, so much so that it often seems like we have little time for ourselves. So, the obvious obstacle to you becoming a daily reader is simply finding the time.

Blogger Thu Vu has some great remedies for the time crunch, one of which is finding small gaps in the day to read a few pages.

Maybe you're a morning person who wakes up bright-eyed and bushy-tailed. If so, then consider getting up a few minutes earlier to fit ten to twenty minutes of reading in before you go to work or school. Many people are more alert and active in the morning, making those spare minutes a perfect time to sneak in some reading.

But what about those of us who just aren't morning people?

Don't worry, if you can't function until you have at least two cups of coffee in the morning, you can simply reverse the pattern. Dedicate ten to twenty minutes after work, before dinner, or even at night when you have all your important things done.

It's also important to remember that as busy as our lives are, they can also be unpredictable. Changing work schedules, family emergencies, car troubles, and a host of other unforeseeable circumstances can throw a monkey wrench into your planned reading time, but those small gaps in the day still exist.

Make sure to always have a book, e-reader, or other reading device in your backpack, purse, or pocket so you can read for a few minutes virtually anywhere. Once you start carrying your reading material with you, you'll begin to get into a daily reading habit.

As your reading habit increases and you learn how to use those small gaps in the day to get in some reading, you'll also find that reading at particular times is helpful. We already discussed how early morning or late evening reading may be good for you, and the more you read, the more you'll start to look forward to your reading times. Reading on your lunch break at work is a good way to put the stress of your job out of your mind for a few minutes, or your fifteen minutes of reading before bed can be a reward for a good day's work.

Setting a specific time to read helps with forming a habit, so trying to find the most consistent time gap during the day is a good way to start this habit.

I'd like to point out here that as you find some time gaps for reading and turn them into a regular reading schedule, feel free to use any media to read. Technology has come a long way since writing was done on papyrus and tomb walls, so take advantage of all the technologies that offer reading content.

You might be more old-school and prefer the feel and smell of paper books, but tablets, laptops, and e-readers, or any combination, are cool too! Whatever helps you develop a regular reading schedule is great.

E-readers, tablets, and laptops are all great modern tools that can enhance your daily reading habit, but be aware that too much tech, especially social media, can impinge on your reading.

No one's judging you for having a Facebook or Twitter account or watching videos of cute cats on YouTube, but too much social media will make you "time poor." The fact is that the average person consumes about 2.4 hours' worth of social media a day, which may not seem like much at first, but it's nearly 17 hours a week, 72 hours a month, and 876 hours a year!

Just think, in all those hours of trying to get likes, you could've been doing some quality reading.

The same goes for TV. Today, TV may be a little low tech compared to smartphones and tablets, but it can be equally distracting. So, be conscious of how much TV you watch and consider reading instead.

For example, let's say you're spending three hours of a Sunday afternoon to watch your favorite football team. You don't need to make it black and white, though—you can do *both*. Read a few pages of your favorite book during halftime to further nurture your daily reading habit.

For many of us, ditching social media and distracting technology is difficult, yet once you do it, you'll soon find how the world of reading opens to you. But as reading opens your mind, it's important to know that there's more than one way to read.

You may be surprised to learn that listening to audiobooks is a great supplement to your daily reading habit. Sure, you may not actually be "reading," but when you're crunched for time, listening to audiobooks or podcasts is a great way to complete that book you've always wanted to read.

And as we've already discussed, time is so often the enemy of our daily reading habit, so anything you can do to maximize your time is great.

Chances are you have a daily commute to work or have to drive to pick up your kids from school or activities, so what better time and place to listen to your favorite audiobook on CD or MP3 than during the drive? And if you're really pressed for time, you can speed up a ten-hour audiobook to 1.8x speed to get it done in five and a half hours.

If you have children, you can involve them in your audiobook experience. Studies have shown that kids who listen to audiobooks have better vocabulary and improved listening skills and are more interested to read, especially if the audiobook is accompanied by a traditional book (Valplowman).

I shouldn't have to point out how listening to audiobooks is a fun activity to do with your children and will help create a stronger familial bond. As you and your family develop your daily reading habits, you'll also become closer.

Organization Is Everything!

Now that we've discussed how important daily reading is and some tools that'll help you develop the habit, let's look at how to organize your reading material. This may not seem very important, but the truth is that organization is a vital part of everything we do, and when it comes to improving your daily reading habit, proper organization will help you with that goal.

The first thing you should do is sit down and start making up physical lists of what you hope to achieve with your new reading habit. Creating a physical list, whether written by hand on a piece of paper or on a word processing document, is a great mental exercise itself. It gets you thinking, and as your list expands, it becomes another thing for you to read.

But you're probably thinking, where do I start with a list of reading goals?

To begin with, keep things simple. Think of some things that interest you and start from there. If you're primarily interested in reading as a way to further your personal development, you might find yourself adding classical literary fiction, well-known self-help books, inspirational spiritual material, or else how-to guides that challenge and educate you.

Try to include wide-ranging topics and even one or two things you've never been attracted to in the past. For example, maybe you would like to learn more about a particular historical period, some fascinating philosophical theory or scientific topic, the biography of a famous and unusual person, beautiful poetry, a political treatise, or an anthropological account of a world and way of life completely different from your own. Once you've made a list of books, you can begin coming up with a list of reading goals that you can then break down into smaller goals—be warned that reading lists tend to grow and grow! But that's a good thing.

Once you have a list of your reading goals, you can segue into creating a list of reading categories.

Just focus on your reading goals, let your mind wander, and in no time, you'll start coming up with some awesome reading categories. If you need a little nudge, consider the following example.

A few years ago, I took a long journey by train across the United States. If you've never done such a trip, it's fairly comfortable but it's also quite long—much longer than it would take to drive. So instead of getting upset by the length of the trip, I decided to take advantage of it by jumping into one of my newly created reading categories—books I was assigned to read in high school but never did.

As I got ready for my long train trip, I dug *Brave New World* by Aldous Huxley, *1984* by George Orwell, and *Animal Farm*, also by Orwell, out of my basement and got ready to read. I was so glad I read those classics and was amazed by what I had missed out on as a teenager. But as the quote by George Bernard Shaw states:

"Youth is the most precious thing in life; it is too bad it has to be wasted on young folks."

You've probably heard that quote before, but it was probably somewhat misquoted as "youth is wasted on the youth," or something like that. Well, when I first learned that this Shaw quote is often misquoted, I decided to come up with another reading category—famous misquoted authors.

For this category, in addition to Shaw, I came up with nineteenth-century German philosopher Friedrich Nietzsche, who is famous for writing "that which doesn't kill us makes us stronger."

And I topped this list off with Niccolò Machiavelli, who in 1532 wrote that it "is better to be feared than loved."

So you can see how, if you follow your nose, one book often leads to another, and a certain genre will introduce you to another, lesser-known genre. Follow your curiosity, keep asking questions, and make connections. In no time you'll start creating vast and fascinating networks of knowledge. Look in the bibliographies of famous books or get interested in who a current author considers as their inspiration. What about authors who are of the same nationality or writing in the same historical period? What about those who completely disagree in some way with the author you've just read?

Consider stepping outside of your comfort zone when choosing material to read. I've never been a fan of Western novels, but after my grandfather died, he left behind a large collection of Zane Grey and Louis L'Amour books. After staring at the box of those books for several months, I begrudgingly decided to add one book of each author to my next list. I eventually ended up reading all twenty-two books in the box and gained a new appreciation of the Western genre in the process—not to mention that it opened up new doors that I wouldn't have gone through otherwise.

Once you have your reading lists and material ready to read, it's important to strategize how to get the most out of your reading.

After you've developed a regular reading habit of some thoughtfully curated reading lists, you'll want to read more and more. Reading is not only fun and mentally challenging, it's also a bit addictive, but in a good way, of course. You'll quickly find that you'll want to get the most reading in, in the limited time you have, but you'll also probably find out that you just can't read as many books and articles as you'd hoped. So, here are a few suggestions to maximize the limited reading time you have.

A really effective method to try is the multiple-booking (pun intended!) method. With this method, you'll read two or more books on one of your lists, or books from different lists, simultaneously.

For example, let's say you're working through a list of novels that were later made into miniseries. So in the fifteen minutes before work, you read a few pages of James Clavell's *Shogun*, and at night before bed, you knock out a chapter of *Centennial* by James Michener.

It also may help to experiment with different technologies when doing the multiple-booking method. Using the same example, you may read on an e-reader or tablet before work or at lunch, but at night, you prefer the feel and smell of a good old-fashioned book!

Another method that may help is researching a book before you read it. There's nothing worse than getting a book and reading about twenty pages of it before you realize it's boring or just not your style. If you're like many people, you'll try to press on and read it since you're already invested. But this usually just means you waste even more time before giving up at some later point in the book, anyway!

In order to avoid this pitfall, first do a little research on the book on Amazon or places like Goodreads. Read the reviews and synopsis and make sure to read the summary on the back of the book. Consider looking at other works by the author, or even read their Wikipedia page to get an idea of where they're coming from. If it's a book you're thinking about purchasing, Amazon and other online booksellers often let you read the table of contents or a few pages for free before purchasing, so make sure to do so. Naturally, being in a physical bookstore makes this trick that much easier!

Garbage in, Garbage out

You've probably heard the term "garbage in, garbage out" at some point in your life. Originally, the term was used in computer science to describe programmers putting bad input into computers and getting bad results in return. The term has also been used to describe bad diets, and in our case, it can be described as your reading diet.

Just as you are what you eat—you are what you read.

With that in mind, it's important to watch how much literary "junk info" you consume. Clay Johnson, author of *The Information Diet*, offers many tips on how to curate your reading diet better by cutting out the junk info.

A useful tip Johnson suggests is keeping notes of all the content you read. You should already be in the practice of doing this after creating your list of goals and reading category lists, so you already have a good start. But you're probably thinking: what's considered junk info?

To be honest, that's not such an easy answer, as one person's junk info may be another person's *War and Peace*. It's true that the value of much of what we read is subjective, but most of us can agree there's some written material we can use less of.

Let's go back to what we discussed earlier about having too much tech in our lives. The very idea of modern technology can distract us from quality reading, but also much of the written material we get via technology is straight-up junk.

You may get several annoying newsletters and meaningless emails in your inbox daily. Maybe some of these newsletters had a purpose at one point in your life, but chances are, you're wasting your time reading through them today. The first step is to set up filters in your emails so you won't even be tempted to read any of these, and once you've done that, take the next step by using technology to help your daily reading.

Johnson mentions several apps and programs that are available to clear the junk info out of your inbox. The app Leave Me Alone automatically unsubscribes you from unsolicited emails, while RescueTime functions as an electronic notebook that tracks what and how much you consume on social media. Other useful electronic tools include AdBlock Plus, Block Plus, and SaneBox.

So how do you deal with news content overload that cuts into your reading time? Using news aggregators work well because they put all the big stories onto one site so you don't have to spend time searching. Prismatic is a site that serves this purpose quite well. You can also use RSS to efficiently organize and streamline your news content.

Another tactic to consider is just checking out the news headlines on various social media sites that you're visiting anyway. LinkedIn Today is a news aggregator available on the popular business/social networking site, while some new search engines offer users new time-saving options.

Topsy and Bottlenose are two new search engines that specialize in finding current trends. So instead of wasting hours searching social media for the latest trends, challenges, and news, try one of these search engines, which will give you more time to focus on your reading lists.

But ultimately, you're the final authority on how much junk info you consume, so consider cutting the "e-cord" by consciously limiting your time online. You can still read books on your e-reader and tablet, as well as listen to audiobooks, so you don't have to go back to the Stone Age just to avoid junk info and maintain your daily reading habit.

A good way to limit your junk info consumption is to take a trip to your local bookstore or library. Yes, both of those places still exist! Visiting used bookstores is an excellent way to find some new reading material and help local businesses. Bookstores in general are also good places to come up with ideas for your future reading lists, as they are often organized by subject matter.

Chapter Takeaways

- Reading is simply one of the best daily habits to cultivate no matter what your personal development goals are. Reading broadens

your horizons, challenges fixed perspectives, deepens your knowledge base, and strengthens your intelligence, comprehension, critical thinking, and empathy ... not to mention it's fun!
- Squeeze in reading where you can, but make a schedule, too, that fits your unique needs. Try different formats (such as eBooks or audiobooks) and remember to keep organized by making lists of your reading goals and making notes about the material you've read.
- Technology can be friend or foe when it comes to reading, so pay attention to whether the internet/devices are serving your reading goals or getting in the way. Be extra mindful of social media apps, as they can really distract you from your reading tasks.
- You can develop your own reading routine over time. The first step is to sit down and start developing concrete lists of what you aim to accomplish with your new reading habit. Making a physical list, whether by hand on a piece of paper or on a word processing document, is a fantastic brain workout in and of itself. It gets you thinking, and as your list grows, it becomes even another thing to read.
- Always be mindful of how much literary "junk info" you are consuming. If you put too much irrelevant junk into your brain, you're gonna get junk in return. A good strategy is to continuously take notes while you are reading and visit bookstores to find exactly what you need and limit confusion.

CHAPTER SIX: Personal Knowledge Management and the Learning Process

Personal knowledge management and lifelong learning have become essential for success in this ever-evolving world. Now more than ever, it is important to develop an understanding of lifelong learning principles and the skills needed for effective personal information management. Developing strategies for curating, organizing, storing, and retrieving content can help us stay ahead of change and take proactive steps toward our educational and career goals. Knowledge management gives us a solid foundation from which we can thrive on our journey toward developing our lifelong passions. Let's learn how to create your very own personal knowledge management system.

Did you know that Babylonian astronomers were using geometry to calculate planetary orbits more than three thousand years ago? Or that medieval scholars were compiling encyclopedias long before the invention of the printing press? Knowledge has always been humanity's most precious resource and one wholly essential for learning. Mankind has always understood that the greatest method to keep improving is to keep learning, which necessitates creating your own personal knowledge management system. So, what on earth is it? Personal knowledge management (PKM) is a collection of processes that a person employs in their regular activities to gather, classify, store, search, retrieve, and share knowledge (Efimova, 2005).

It is important to understand that knowledge management isn't just about collecting and organizing information. It's not just about hoarding knowledge. The ultimate goal should always be about using knowledge in a way that enhances learning and personal growth. This can involve regularly reflecting on new knowledge gained and how it relates to our existing understanding, as well as actively seeking out opportunities to apply this knowledge in practical ways. Before we get into the process of managing knowledge, it is important that we understand exactly why doing so is essential in the first place.

In 1885, German psychologist Hermann Ebbinghaus published a groundbreaking study on memory and learning. In his research, he found that people have a tendency to forget information over time. The "forgetting curve" is one of the most well-known concepts to come out of

Ebbinghaus's research. It shows that humans forget roughly 50 percent of new information within an hour, and 70 percent within a day (Shakow, 1930). The curve demonstrates how learned knowledge fades from our memories over time unless we take steps to preserve it there. We know the steepest decline in memory occurs shortly after learning, so therefore it's critical to review what you've learned as soon as possible. But how do you do that if you don't know exactly where the information is?

Personal knowledge management is truly your knight in shining armor here! It enables you to delegate the task of remembering. Instead of remembering all the facts, you simply need to remember that you know it and that you know where to find it. Think of it as a system that will allow you to organize and store ideas and references as building blocks. Then, whenever you need to start a project, you just select and assemble the necessary building components to create a finished artwork. Therefore, the less time and energy you spend on the building blocks, the more time you have to actually create something beautiful.

There's really no doubt about it: We live in an age of complete information overload. It seems like every day you wake up and are faced with a chiming laptop signaling to us that there's ten more articles on the "benefits of guided meditation" that you need to look at right now! I mean, you probably only wanted to look at a few for your seminar next week but now are suddenly feeling anxious and overwhelmed at the thought of missing something super important! Your phone suddenly pings, pulling you out of anxious thoughts. Oh great! There are four new blog posts, a podcast, and a book recommendation. Isn't this just *lovely*!

In situations like these, it's very easy to fall victim to information overload, sometimes known as information anxiety, if you do not have a system in place that filters out the noise and keeps only what is relevant and insightful (Simperl et al., 2010). But how do we do that? You guessed it! By having a knowledge management system in place! With so much information out there, it's no wonder people are having panic attacks before routine presentations (I've had many).

Most of us are getting lost in the internet's rabbit hole of information in the guise of "research." We are saving, staring, and bookmarking posts, notes, and random links that we need to go back through and organize. Having a system in place is going to help us get rid of whatever is inconsequential and keep only what is necessary for future reference.

One of the great things about knowledge is that it builds on itself. The more you know, the easier it is to learn new things. This is because you can connect new information to existing knowledge, making it easier to remember and understand.

This process is known as compounding, and it's one of the most efficient ways to learn. In fact, studies have shown that students who are able to connect new information to existing knowledge are more likely to retain that information (Hailikari et al., 2007). Rereading a book you already read ten years ago will help you learn more today. This happens because you connect the concepts to a wider body of information.

The notes you are gathering, starring, and bookmarking will create new combinations of ideas for you to unlock. You might have observed artists, writers, and all sorts of creatives do this. Their ability to connect present moments to ideas decades old to create something new for us is what makes all art forms so unique. Thus, if you don't have a management system in place, it will be really challenging to keep track of all your ideas and notes (plus, you'd probably forget everything and connecting anything would be impossible). If you're unable to remember prior knowledge and ideas, how on earth are you going to connect it to something new?

Now that we have established how important it is to have a personal knowledge management system, it's time to unravel the three main steps to creating the best PKM system that will assist in your learning.

Gather and Capture

Meet Kevin, a man with varied tastes. Passionate about work but just as equally passionate about life. He loves immersing himself in the fascinating and often fantastical world of literature, video games, movies, clandestine encounters, vague memories of tantalizing conversations, and lessons learned. He wants to incorporate the knowledge he has gathered over the years into something practical, something meaningful. He is intelligent and compassionate, but he feels like he hasn't made any discernible progress in his life. He often wonders why.

You see, Kevin, like me, is very lazy. He thinks that he does not need to write anything down or take notes because he relies solely on his brain to save information. You remember the forgetting curve, right? Well, Kevin is not immune to it; nobody is (unless you're a superhero—then maybe you are).

Making it a habit to save any information or ideas you believe to be helpful or inspiring when you come across them is the first step in personal knowledge management. This is known as creating a "capture habit" in the context of David Allen's Getting Things Done system for organizing and managing tasks. The ultimate capture goal is to be able to quickly save these items wherever you find them. Don't be concerned with including details. They can later be filtered and organized.

For instance, a few "capture" inboxes that can help you in creating your own are as follows:

- My tiny research notebook (that I only use for class), jam-packed with notes
- My fluffy pink notebook that I keep close by when I work
- An iOS note that I can add to using Siri and access from the home screen of my iPhone
- The same note app on my laptop
- Planners that I have personalized on Canva

Anything I believe I might wish to use as a source for my work goes into these inboxes. In the previous week, I've recorded:

- Articles that I want to cite in my own work (like this one)
- Ideas for writing styles derived from discussions with clients
- Screenshots of websites and visual designs that I loved
- A study on narrative-driven video games that I found fascinating

If you have a set way of capturing things, it will make it easier for you to take notes on the side and save things without having to divert your attention. A key challenge that you might face in this stage is applying and sustaining these practices as an ongoing set of habits. Remember,

habits play a very vital role in true lifelong learning and freedom (Bernacer et al., 2015). William James, author of *The Principles of Psychology*, discussed habits and their importance in achieving happiness and success. Water, he claims, is the best analogy for how habits work. Water "hollows for itself a channel that grows wider and deeper and, after ceasing to flow, resumes, when it flows again, the course traced by itself previously." You now have the ability to change that course. You now have the ability to swim.

One good strategy to keep yourself on track is developing a system for gathering information. This might include setting up Google Alerts for topics you're interested in, subscribing to relevant RSS feeds, or following certain social media accounts. The key is to make it as easy as possible for you to find interesting articles, blog posts, and other pieces of information while also helping you sustain this habit. Otherwise, you'll quickly become overwhelmed by the sheer volume of information out there and will want to give up.

Whether you're reading a book, a blog, or an article, it's always a good idea to come up with a system for taking notes that works for you—bullet points, highlighting key phrases, using a traditional journal, or making edits on soft copies. For example, when I read articles online, I like to look for a PDF that I can download. This allows me to quickly highlight the main points as well as add comments. I can then easily go back and access the key information without wasting any time skimming the article once again. Similarly, if I am reading a book, I prefer to keep a hefty stack of vibrant sticky notes on hand so that I can make my book look like a Piñata (it helps make the most boring of textbooks appealing). Oh, and it helps me add my own ideas to the key points I want to highlight.

Once you have a system for gathering information and a preferred method for note taking, you need a way to organize it so that you can easily find what you're looking for later on. If your desk is anything like mine, it's covered in Post-It Notes, half-finished to-do lists, and crumpled up pieces of paper with ideas, dreams, and passions that just won't fit anywhere else. In other words, it's a hot mess. You've probably tried every organization system out there, from the bullet journal to good old-fashioned pen and paper. But somehow, nothing ever seems to stick.

One effective way to organize knowledge is by tagging your information with keywords. For example, if you come across an article about the benefits of meditation, you might tag it with "meditation," "mindfulness," and "wellness." You can also organize your information using folders. For example, you might create a folder for health-related articles, another folder for articles about productivity, and so on. You can use physical or digital journals. (Canva has some pretty great options! Plus, you can customize your own. It truly is journal heaven!)

Organize What You've Captured

In an age when we're constantly bombarded with information, it's more important than ever to know how to label, tag, and organize it. After all, if you can't find the information you need when you need it, what good is it? Here are a few tips to help you get started.

First, think about how you want to access the information. Do you want to be able to search for it by keyword, or do you want to be able to browse through it? That will dictate how you label it. For example, if you're labeling a file on your computer, you might want to use a system of keywords so that you can easily find it when you do a search. On the other hand, if you're putting together a binder of information, you might want to use a more organizational system, such as dividing it into sections.

Whether you're organizing your home computer files or adding labels to a client's presentation, it's important to know how to tag information correctly. The process of tagging information is simple: You just need to choose a system that makes sense for the task at hand and then label each piece of information accordingly. For example, if you're organizing a music collection, you might want to tag each song by its genre, artist, and release date.

On the other hand, if you're looking to organize your research for your final-year thesis, you might want to tag and label studies and information in accordance with the variables you are studying. For instance, you are exploring empathy and attitudes toward mental illness in young adults. Tagging everything you find in relevance to "empathy," "empathy in young adults," "attitudes toward mental illness," and "attitudes toward mental illness in young adults" will greatly benefit you in streamlining your thoughts.

Once you've chosen a system, simply label each piece of information accordingly and then use the tags to help you find what you're looking for later on. With a little practice, tagging can be an invaluable way to keep your thoughts and materials neatly organized.

Secondly, make sure your labels are clear and concise. This isn't the time to be clever or cutesy—you want to be able to understand your labels at a glance. Use language that is straightforward and easy to grasp. Finally, don't be afraid to change your system if it's not working for you. Reviewing, rewriting, and repurposing should be your most important PKM practice. As your needs change, so, too, should the way you label and organize your information, as well as the information itself. Any new information added to the system should be revisited after a couple days. It will help you in getting rid of the fluff and expose the juiciest of details.

The goal is to make your life easier, not harder—so don't hesitate to experiment until you find a system and the precise information that works for you.

You should do the following while organizing the information you have gathered:

1. Start by identifying the key points of the material you're trying to learn. What are the most important concepts? What are the main takeaways? Once you've identified the key points, try to find real-life examples that illustrate those concepts. This step will help you better understand the concept and its relevance to what you're learning. For example, you recently came across an article on emotion regulation.

    You know that regulating emotions is essential for maintaining healthy relationships, managing stress effectively, and achieving success in both personal and professional realms, but what exactly is it? Can you think of some real-life examples? Let's say you're at a party and you see your ex with someone new. You feel a twinge of jealousy, but instead of letting it spiral out of control, you take a deep breath and remember that you're happy in your own life. That's an example of emotion regulation in action.

Or let's say you get passed over for a big promotion at work. You're feeling frustrated and disappointed, but instead of throwing a temper tantrum or quitting on the spot, you decide to put your head down and work even harder. Again, that's emotion regulation. Examples like these stemming from your own lived experiences can help you with learning and implementing mindfulness techniques in life as well as tell you whether or not you need to keep this information for future reference.

2. Make sure you deeply understand the material. It's not enough just to be able to regurgitate information; you need to be able to explain how and why certain things work. When you can do that, you'll be much better equipped to determine the relevancy of the information and get rid of what you don't need. Let's go back to the example of emotion regulation.

There are several different theories about why emotion regulation works, but one of the most prominent is the idea that it helps us stay grounded in our reality. When we're experiencing negative emotions, it's easy to get lost in them and forget what's really going on around us. But if we can regulate our emotions, we can keep ourselves from getting too caught up in our own heads. This allows us to perspective-take, which is an essential part of empathy. So not only does emotion regulation work help us feel better in the moment, but it also helps us be more understanding and compassionate toward others (Gillespie, Beech, 2017)

3. Delete everything you no longer find useful or relevant. Create context by making notes to your future self. (Why did you save this? Does this inspire you? If yes, in what way? Are there any parts that you'd like to use in the future? How is this going to help me achieve my goals? Remove everything you feel is no longer useful.) To make finding and filtering in your management system easier, include metadata such as tags. You should then move the sifted data to a more permanent location where you can easily access it whenever you need to.

Items from my own notes, for example, are frequently relocated to different folders for reference articles or project planning

(Inspiration for My Book, Travel Ideas, Books Ideas, Art Inspo, etc.). Therefore, whenever I'm in need of something, I go to that specific folder and find everything I need in there. This way, I can actually use my knowledge instead of it being lost in sticky notes and random scribblings that don't make any sense.

Process Your Information and Compound Your Knowledge

The Zettelkasten method is a notetaking system that was developed by German sociologist and economist Niklas Luhmann. The system is based on the principle of "the larger the net, the more fish you will catch." The aim is to capture ideas and connect them with one another. It is composed of three essential elements: slips of paper, a filing system, and a mind map. The slips of paper are used to record ideas, thoughts, and information. These slips are then sorted into different categories and filed accordingly. The mind map is used to visualize the relationships between different ideas.

It beautifully showcases all the three essential elements of a PKM system: The slips of paper signify the gathering and the capturing stage, the filing system signifies the organizing, and the final is the mind map or the compounding of knowledge. This stage consists of rigorously studying and analyzing the information to find patterns that either align with what we already know, or deviate from it. This is the true essence of learning—combining different ideas to give birth to something new. For, my friend, the time has come to actually make some magic happen!

All your notes up until now should strictly center around specific themes that are tagged and labeled as such. This will allow you to quickly connect and reframe your notes because each one only contains a single theme or a concept. Don't let the word "connect" scare you. You just need to critically review and analyze the information to establish links between different concepts. Let's go back to that example of organizing your research for your final-year thesis, where you tagged and labeled studies in relevance to "empathy," "empathy in young adults," "attitudes toward mental illness," and "attitudes toward mental illness in young adults."

Anyone who has ever undertaken research is aware that a good chunk of it involves establishing a correlation between all the variables being studied. A correlation simply means a relationship or an association between two or more concepts or variables. Here, for example, you will try to see if "empathy" connects to "attitudes toward mental illness." Is there a link between "empathy" and "attitudes" in general? Does one make you think of the other? When you refer to your "empathy" notes, are there any other notes that you wish to see? Feel a connection brewing? These are important questions to ponder during this stage, as this is where you will establish all links.

Following are some special strategies that can help you in this endeavor.

- Make bridge notes to connect ideas that are only noticeably connected in the second view. Simply explain why there is a relationship or an association so that your future self does not have to figure it out on their own again. Let's say you come across an article on the relationship between "perspective-taking" and "attitudes toward mental health." At first glance, you might think that this might not be relevant to the research you are conducting because it does not show an obvious link. When it comes to research, sometimes we will not find exactly what we are looking for; thus, it becomes important to establish links where there aren't any.
- Looking at perspective-taking closely, you will see that we can bridge the gap between our two variables by looking at perspective-taking as an essential component of empathy, for it is our ability to take on someone's else's perspective that shows how empathetic we truly are (you can later find research to support this). You can then take this and connect it to "attitudes toward mental illness." Congratulations! You have essentially created

a bridge note! You have bridged the gap between "perspective-taking" and "attitudes toward mental illness." You have discovered that these two ideas are noticeably connected in the second view, and you have made notes to explain exactly why. Your future self is going to thank you for this!

- Develop index notes to organize ideas by topic. Creating index notes is a great way to organize your ideas and keep track of the information you need for a project or paper. Create an index note for each topic that you are studying. For example, you can create one for "empathy" and another for "attitudes toward mental illness."
- As you come across relevant information in your reading, add it to the appropriate card. When you're ready to start writing, you can quickly find the information you need by consulting your index notes. When connecting concepts, you can just link it back to the index note. For example, rather than noting ten connections on ten notes of "empathy" and "attitudes toward mental illness," each note that connects the two concepts can just refer to the index notes. Way less messy!
- Develop topic notes that take a broader view to group relevant notes together. These can help you lay bare all the connections between your ideas. You can add your own spin to them and make them really unique. Taking from the research example I mentioned above, here we can create a category called, "empathy and

attitudes toward mental illness." Or we can have separate categories for baking (kringles and Danishes), gaming (shooters and narratives), or books (fantasy and adventure), or whatever project you are working on.

As crucial as it is to establish connections, it is also beneficial to frequently review your analyses and lessons learned so that they can embed themselves in your long-term memory, where they will be most helpful.

Another helpful strategy for processing information is progressive summarization. It is a reading comprehension strategy that involves readers making increasingly detailed summaries of what they have read as they progress through a text. This strategy can be particularly helpful when reading long or complex texts, as it allows readers to keep track of the main ideas and keep their understanding of the text focused. This is an excellent technique for establishing a successful PKM system.

Enter Martha. She has to review a paper for her history class, but she hasn't the slightest clue how she is going to get through this giant piece of text in two days! Well, we have some good news for Martha. All she needs to do is progressively summarize. She has already captured and gathered the information, even organized all the concepts into key learnings, but then why is she having so much trouble starting? What most of us forget is that we need to constantly revisit, rewrite, and repurpose the knowledge we have gathered if we ever hope to actually learn something new.

With progressive summarization, Martha starts by making a brief overview of the text as a whole with the help of the key points she has already extracted. She adds more points, eliminates some. Then, she moves on to making more detailed summaries of each section or chapter. Finally, she summarizes the newly repurposed key points of the entire text in a single paragraph. By taking the time to progressively summarize a text, she ensures that she has a clear and concise understanding of its main ideas and can readily link them now.

One of the great things about linking concepts is that it gives you a chance to combine different ideas and see what happens. For example, you could take two completely disparate concepts and see how they interact with each other. Maybe you've always been interested in ancient history, but you've also been curious about quantum mechanics. Why not try to write a paper that explores the connection between the two? Or maybe you're a big fan of both romance novels and crime thrillers. Could you write a novel that combines elements of both genres? The possibilities are endless. So don't be afraid to experiment and see what happens when you mix different ideas together. You might just come up with something great!

In essence, it's crucial to invest in your thoughts; invest in your ideas and thinking; engage in your curiosity; and pull out that notebook full of little tidbits on how to bake, how to sew, how to paint, how to design, how to write, how to literally become anything that you have ever wanted to be. Start giving meaning to the knowledge you have gathered. When you give your knowledge context and meaning, you begin to see compound interest. It's the same as a lot of good behaviors.

It can take some time at first to get into it and make it part of your routine. But once you've done that, you usually feel more content, as if you know more, and you're glad you started in the first place. Go grab that notebook, open that folder, and start right now. Walk this path with me as I guide you like Gandalf guided Frodo through the treacherous landscape of Middle-earth. We shall embark on our very own journey of challenged productivity, capture and gather knowledge, process and organize it, and let inspiration be our compass to avoid the fires of Mount Doom.

Chapter Takeaways

- Personal knowledge management (PKM) is a set of processes that a person uses in their daily activities to collect, categorize, store, search for, retrieve, and share knowledge.

- Creating a "capture habit" is the first step in personal knowledge management, which is important for lifelong learning and freedom. A capture habit involves quickly saving any helpful or inspiring information or ideas that are come across. This can be done by setting up Google Alerts, subscribing to RSS feeds, following social media accounts, etc.
- Once information is gathered, it needs to be properly labeled and organized using a system that makes sense for the task at hand. This will make it easier to find later on when needed. The goal is to make your life easier by understanding and implementing the techniques learned from gathering this information.
- The Zettelkasten method is a notetaking system developed by German sociologist Niklas Luhmann that helps you capture ideas and connect them with one another. It has three essential elements: slips of paper, a filing system, and a mind map. The slips of paper are used to record ideas, thoughts, and information, which are then sorted into different categories and filed accordingly.
- The mind map is used to visualize the relationships between different ideas. In order to make connections between concepts, you can use special strategies like bridge notes or progressive summarization. Bridge notes can be used to connect ideas, index notes to organize ideas, and topic notes to group relevant information or notes together.

CHAPTER SEVEN: Create Your Own Personal Syllabus and Reflective Learning

Working deeply and deliberately on a passion goal isn't always easy, especially when you don't have an outside authority or syllabus to guide your learning process. Yet the best way to truly master a topic—whether it be a new language or skill set—is to come up with your own personal syllabus and use deep work to stick with it.

Go beyond simply reading through tutorials; try out actions associated with the topic, apply what you're learning in different contexts, and take time for reflection throughout the journey. Remember: having an effective syllabus that allows room for flexibility can make all the difference when it comes to engaging with deep work.

One of the biggest goals of most people in life is personal and professional development. But why do some manage to get so far, while others remain in the same place without progressing in their lives and careers? Is luck the key to success? Or maybe fate?

The secret to being successful in life and profession is *not* in chance, but in the strategies of action and in the possibilities that each one creates for himself. When obstacles appear in the way, not everyone is prepared to remove them and move on. And this process of overcoming and learning needs to be constant.

You don't need to wait for some external institution to impose a curriculum on you—you can set your own goals and create a program for development. Some people enroll in courses or degrees or wait for their employers to send them to get specialist training. But others don't need this permission and can take their own growth and development into their own hands. Creating a personal syllabus is the ideal way to achieve this ambition.

Designing Your Personal Syllabus

Let's take the real-life example of Harry, who recently graduated with a degree in computer sciences. Harry started applying for entry-level roles with several software companies. However, he is still confused on how to get on with his career. Harry's love for computers goes back to his childhood, and he has always dreamed of becoming a computer engineer. He knows that to get a job at the right place, he needs to develop expertise in at least one programming language.

However, he isn't prepared to sit back and wait for the companies to call him. He wants to take control of his own personal and professional development. How can self-learning help Harry land his dream job?

Creating a personal syllabus is a commitment to your own development. It is a plan that systematizes various actions to be taken so that you achieve a certain goal through personal and professional development. In other words, it's a roadmap for you to get from where you are now to where you want to be. Or, more broadly, to become who you would like to be.

As it is a real written document with goals and deadlines, your personal syllabus helps you maintain focus. By sticking to strategically considered steps, you don't get carried away by random distractions and you are not derailed by unforeseen events.

Creating your own syllabus is not easy, but it pays huge dividends for the time you invest in your personal growth. Before proceeding to set goals for your personal development, you need to know which skills you need to develop, as well as adopt a *growth mindset*. Some believe that they are born with a certain number or type of skills that can never be changed, which implies that learning new skills is outside their comfort zone and impossible. This is a *fixed mindset*. However, with a growth mindset, you accept challenges and embrace new experiences because you fundamentally believe you are capable of change and growth. This means you see setbacks as a way to grow, and you reflect on ways to use your skills to improve your deficits.

While creating a personal syllabus, it is important to understand what skills need to be developed or honed in order to cope with a job or reach a new professional level.
Taking the example of Harry, he knows that Python is in demand and wants to be a Python programmer, and he even studied the topic at the university. However, he is still short of the skills required to land his dream job.

He sees that it's definitely worth assessing his current skills accurately, reinforcing the basics, and choosing a course for Basic to Advanced Python. The skills that you need will naturally be different, but it's up to you to prioritize the skills needed, perhaps based on your dream job's requirements or the skills requested by job vacancies.

Set SMART Goals and Create a Mind Map

When building a training plan, you need to start with goals. See where you want to be in a year and what position you'd like to take. Go to LinkedIn or another job portal and write out the requirements and responsibilities from the relevant vacancies. Opposite each non-recurring item, note what skills you already possess and what is yet to be added to your portfolio of competencies. Then see how you can develop the skills you need—whether it be paid courses, YouTube videos, expert blogs, or hands-on tasks.

Once you have identified the areas and skills you need to work on, think about what you want to achieve in your studies and work. Experts advise using the SMART model when setting goals. According to the model, goals should be specific, measurable, achievable, meaningful, and time limited.

Your personal learning syllabus could include goals such as:

- An "I want to learn x . . ." learning goal. For example, "to become confident in my public presentation and speaking skills" or "to write clearer and more concise emails."
- An "I will learn via . . ." strategy. This could mean watching Udemy courses, signing up for speaking skills training, or taking part in amateur dramatics, for instance.
- An "I will know that I've been successful when . . ." measurement. This could be receiving positive feedback on a presentation. Or it could be as simple as recognizing that you feel

less stressed when you're speaking on the phone.

For example, the goal to "learn Python" sounds vague. It is better to formulate it like this: "Learn to work with advanced Python language, get a certification, and find a job in an international company." When you understand why you need to learn something, the goal motivates you and learning comes easier.

It's often helpful to break down your long-term objective into smaller steps. Following this and other golden rules of goal setting can help you stay focused and increase your chances of success.

Make a List of Resources

We are all different. Therefore, we do not think and learn in the same way. To maximize your learning, try to (re)discover your learning style. Your learning style defines how you learn best. There are many theories about learning styles, but the simplest and most concrete is the one that stems directly from our sensory channels:

- The visual profile (sight)
- Auditory profile (touch)
- The kinesthetic profile (smell, hearing, and taste)

There are many websites that offer tests to identify your cognitive profile—which, incidentally, may change over time. You could have been more visual as a child but are more auditory as an adult. Knowing your cognitive profile will allow you to know which tools are most appropriate for your development and which profile(s) you should develop.

For instance:

- If you are more visual, read books, check infographics, watch videos, etc.
- If you are more auditory: listen to podcasts, read aloud, watch videos, etc.
- If you are more kinesthetic: take notes, role play, materialize concepts, etc.

We are lucky to live in a world where knowledge is just a click away, and we have access to a world of information online. Vary the media to stay motivated, adapt them to your availability, and combine several sources of information. In Harry's case, he might find that he most enjoys learning via online multimedia courses, where he can watch videos and interact with others on forums.

To read	**To listen**	**Others**
Books	Podcasts	Apps
Magazines	Videos	Groups
Newsletters	Webinar	
eBooks	Conferences	
White Papers		

You can also use this resource list to find all the resources for your personal syllabus.

Create a Schedule and Deadlines

Learning is not something you can just shove into your life and hope for the best. Learning should instead be the sun around which all your other activities orbit like planets. Do not forget that you are learning to improve your life—what could be more important than that?
When choosing formats and duration of training, take into account your work schedule, family circumstances, seasonality, and other factors that may affect the implementation of your personal syllabus.

Make it clear yet flexible. Once you have chosen courses, add them to your schedule. Mark business trips, holidays, and family duties in the calendar. Then mark the dates associated with the training: the beginning and end of studies, the days you need to attend classes, the deadlines for submitting papers and tests, and so on. Also consider the days and times of day when you are most energetic and efficient.

Create a time frame for each goal. What are you going to do today, tomorrow, next week, and six months from now to reach your goal? Make sure you apply time management and learn how to properly budget your time.

Create a daily routine. Change doesn't happen by itself. And it needs to happen more than once—i.e., your learning needs to be habitual, day in and day out. Consistency is key.

It is important that your short-term goals align with your long-term career goals. For example, in a couple years, Harry might want to go into Python consulting. Does he need to deepen his knowledge in the language itself or master new tools and programs? Does he need to improve communication skills or learn how to negotiate? This will help him prioritize learning, systematically move toward his goal, and not try to do everything at once.

A time-based target date, deadline, or schedule is important when creating a personal syllabus. This could be your ultimate learning and development goal or mission statement, or it could be stages along the way. For example, "I will learn x new Python skill by August, and then focus on developing a skill by the end of the year." There needs to be a process of regular review, evaluation, and, if necessary, a complete reset. While this is happening, you can continue to seek out the training resources you need to move your career along.

Setting benchmarks and tracking progress is the very process that positively affects your level of motivation. As already mentioned, in the process of learning, you will not immediately begin to receive practical results, which means that there's a risk of giving up in the early stages—unless you are vigilant and prepared and track your progress.

Tracking should be understood primarily as keeping a diary. You write down what you studied as well as how much time it took. Document everything. In a few weeks, it will be possible to draw certain conclusions based on this information. You will learn to identify trends, understand your strengths and weaknesses, and recognize bad and good habits. In Harry's case, he can combine this with feedback he receives from tutors on a formal course, or ask mentors for their advice on how he is progressing.

Along with reminders and rewards, enlist family and friends to help you with your self-learning plan. It can be difficult on your own, but if you enlist a friend or relative to help you stick to your plan, you'll feel obligated to complete the task and feel guilty if you don't. In fact, the more people you rope in, the more likely you are to be asked about your progress. These simple questions may be just what you need to stay on top of your plan. For Harry, knowing that his younger cousin is studying the same course brings just enough of a sense of competition to keep him on his toes and remind him what his priorities are.

Following a personal syllabus and achieving your goals will only benefit you; however, overcoming difficulties when you don't feel like committing or working is the hardest part.

You can create your own learning plan based on the steps, or follow this template from Dr. Bernard Bull (Personal Learning Plan Template—Google Docs).

The Gibbs Method of Reflecting on Your Learning Journey

Finally, no personal syllabus is complete without enough time and space dedicated to stopping and evaluating your progress—after all, this is the only way you can make course corrections and reappraise your goals and methods.

Self-reflection is deliberately pausing to consider and contemplate your progress. It takes conscious awareness and a whole lot of honesty. In the process of self-reflection, a person seems to look into a mirror and describe everything that he sees in it. This is a method of evaluating yourself, your methods of work, and your learning processes.

In psychology, self-reflection is an excellent tool for evaluating the effectiveness of any approach you're taking toward self-improvement. This is a powerful way to develop as a person, to make yourself better, and to achieve significant success in life. It's like stopping on a journey to check if you're still en route to your destination and reminding yourself of the map you're following.

Reflective learning consists of becoming aware of your own learning process—it is a kind of meta learning. Being reflective in your learning implies thinking about what and how you're learning to understand yourself and your learning better. You can reflect on:

- Your understanding of the material. For example, how well you understand certain concepts.
- Your understanding of how to implement what you've learned. For example, when and how you can use a certain formula.
- Your learning process. For example, how well certain learning strategies work for you.
- Your abilities, preferences, and thoughts. For example, how difficult or enjoyable you find a certain topic.
- Your goals. For example, where and when you plan to implement something that you've learned, and what you hope to achieve by doing so.

When doing all this, you can use various questions to guide your reflection, as shown in the examples above, and the following are some specific questions that you might benefit from using:

- Which parts of the material do I understand well? How do I know that I understand this material well?
- Which parts of the material do I struggle with? What specifically am I struggling with, and why?
- Which learning techniques do I feel are helpful? Why do I feel that they are helpful?
- Which learning techniques do I feel are unhelpful? Why do I feel that they are unhelpful?
- Are there any changes that I can make to my learning process to make it better for me?
- Should I ask someone else for help, either with my reflection or with my learning? If so, then what should I ask about, and who is a good person to ask this?

Gibbs Reflective Cycle for Self-Reflection

The Gibbs Reflective Cycle is a simple six-stage process that can help you reflect on your experiences at work. You'll learn what is working well and what could be better, and develop a plan of action to minimize weaknesses. This model was first described by Professor Graham Gibbs in his 1998 book, *Learning by Doing: A Guide to Teaching and Learning Methods*.

This theory was partly inspired by the Kolb Learning Cycle, which was in turn inspired by the work of Kurt Lewin. This model consists of six steps:

The first three steps focus on events during the analyzed experience. The last three steps focus on how you can take advantage of the experience so that you can anticipate similar situations in the future that you will encounter.

This series of processes is a worthwhile career skill to learn. You can use it to evaluate performance in your professional environment, but it's also a great model to use if you're training subordinates or colleagues to improve their skills in a particular area.

Description

Describe in detail the experience to be reflected on, including: where you were at the time of the incident, who else was involved/there, why you were there, what you did, what other people did, in what context the experience occurred, what happened, what your role in this experience was, what the role of others was, and what the result of that experience was.

Feelings

Identify and examine the reactions, feelings, and thoughts that emerged during the incident. Try to be honest about how you feel and think even though this may not be easy. The following questions can help you explain the feelings and thoughts involved in the reflected experience:

- How did I feel when the incident started?
- What was on my mind at that time?
- How did the incident affect my feelings? If certain feelings arose during the event, what caused them? Why is that? How do the other people involved in it affect how I feel?
- How did my feelings affect my actions and thoughts on the experience?
- How do I feel about the outcome of the incident?
- Looking back on the experience now, have my feelings changed from before? How do I feel about it now?

Evaluation

Try to evaluate or make a judgment about what has happened. Consider what was good and what was bad about the experience. What went well and what didn't go well in your experience? What makes you think so?

Analysis

In this section, thoroughly examine and understand the influencing factors in the situation/experience and explore various ways to improve it or develop it for the better. In conducting the analysis, try to describe the event/experience you are reflecting on and explore each part separately. Identify the key aspects that contributed to this experience, and the possible explanations for each (how and why). For example, consider aspects of communication or time management that may play an important role in the final outcome of the experience you reflect on.

Also describe any ideas or theories (if any) that you think could help you understand the situation. Are there any ideas, theories, or approaches that could help you improve on this key aspect in the future?

Compare this experience with other experiences that you think are similar or related or can be compared to the literature you read.

These questions can help you analyze each of the components:

- What went well?
- What have I done well?
- What things have other people done well?
- What went wrong or unexpected?
- In what ways did I or someone else contribute to the incident?
- Are there any other experiences that are similar to this one? What can I learn from

these other experiences in relation to understanding the experiences I am reflecting on now?
- Are there any ideas, theories, or literature that can help me understand and develop a solution to this situation?

Conclusion

The difference between this stage and the evaluation stage is that at this stage, you have seen the incident from various perspectives and should have a lot of information to support your assessment. At this stage, too, you already have insight into the contribution of your actions/behaviors and others to the consequences of an event. Remember that the purpose of reflection is to learn from experience.

Without detailed analysis and honesty in conducting exploration, we will not be able to see the various aspects that influence our judgment, and this inhibits true learning. In your conclusion, it is important to be aware of the following:

- Were you actually able to do anything different during this experience?
- What have you learned from this experience?
- If the experience you are reflecting on is a positive one, also discuss whether you would do the same if this experience were repeated to ensure a positive outcome. Also consider if

there is anything else you would like to change to improve your output/results.
- If the experience was a negative one, also explain how you could prevent/avoid it in the future and how you can make sure that the experience or an aspect of the experience does not happen again.

Action Plan

At this stage, think about what you will do if you encounter a similar incident in the future. Would you do something different, or would you do the same thing? Is there something important here for you to learn? Or is there any training you need to take? Do you need advice or input from a supervisor? At this stage, the reflection cycle tentatively ends, but if a similar incident is experienced again, the learner will re-enter the next cycle of reflection.

For Harry, his self-reflection takes place with bigger events (such as failing a major course module) to smaller, more everyday ones (such as wondering if it's better to study certain material before or after lunch each day). The idea is never to be punitive or judgmental; rather, you remain curious and keep asking essentially two questions: Is what I'm doing working? What can I do that will work even better?

Deep Work

Deep working is working without distraction on a hard task. The type of work that constitutes deep work will vary from person to person and workload to workload. Although most people are familiar with the sentiment of deep work and can probably even point to several times in their life when they have entered this flow state and produced work on this level of high focus, the truth is, deep work is a dying art.

The ability to harness your focus to complete cognitively demanding tasks is becoming less and less common due to our increasingly distracting environments. Emails, social media, and messaging are at our fingertips, and the cost of these convenient luxuries is that we are losing our ability to focus for prolonged periods. The good news is that you can undo this damage and regain control of your focus with the principles of deep work.

Deep Work Versus Shallow Work

The term *deep work* was coined by Cal Newport, a computer science professor and best-selling author (clearly someone with high levels of focus), in his book *Deep Work*. In the book, he highlights two different working methods: deep work and shallow work.

Shallow work consists of tasks that take up the majority of our time and energy. They are the tasks that keep us busy and, as Cal Newport puts it, "they keep the lights on." Checking your emails, having meetings, invoicing clients, and making your PowerPoint presentation visually appealing are all examples of shallow work. Are they important? Of course, but they aren't the difference makers, and they're not the things that will lead to creation and innovation. This work won't produce results that will get you a promotion or solve a company-wide problem; it is quite simply just work we must do.

Because this type of work is not cognitively demanding, we can balance it quite easily with distractions. If you are midway through checking your emails and suddenly your phone buzzes and you need to reply to a few texts, you'll find it relatively easy to switch back to focusing on your emails when those texts have been sent. While these tasks require attention, the attention is not intense, and you can flit between tasks because of how little brain power is required to complete them.

In contrast, deep work requires focus. Lots of focus! It requires brain power and a distraction-free environment. Think of tasks like coding, creative writing, and complex problem-solving. The kind of tasks that you could lose all sense of time while completing . . . if only you didn't keep checking your phone. This is the type of work that produces quality, and it's becoming increasingly rare.

Let's give another example: You have been deep working for twenty minutes on researching a new article. Your phone buzzes and you begin to answer a few texts. When you try to go back to focusing on your research, you can't. You lose the momentum of your focus, and the discomfort required to re-enter the deep-work state only makes further distractions more appealing. So you decide to open your emails and complete some other (shallow) tasks. Within thirty minutes, you're on YouTube, watching a video of a dog trying to carry two tennis balls in its mouth at the same time. Okay, that might have gotten a little bit specific, but hopefully you get the point: Cognitively demanding tasks cannot be maintained with distractions.

One of the biggest advantages of being able to deep work often and for longer is this: not many people can. The Western world is so bombarded with high-dopamine distractions that it's no wonder we are losing our ability to concentrate and put distractions aside for even relatively short periods of time. While this is a problem on a societal level, it offers huge opportunities on the individual level. If you can train yourself to work free of disturbances on things that are difficult to do, you will have a huge competitive advantage over those who cannot. If you can produce in an hour what others produce in a day, you will be more successful than those people.

The ability to focus and avoid distraction and interruption is fast becoming a superpower. However, you don't need to be bitten by a radioactive spider or go through secret military experiments to get it. What you need to do is much scarier than that: Make yourself comfortable with being uncomfortable. Learning how to deep work is a great way to practice this skill.

Okay, so we've established that deep work is important. Now here is the fun bit:
How can you get better at deep working and make it a more consistent part of your life? One of the fundamental steps to increasing the amount of deep work you can achieve is simple, and we've actually just done it—we've defined it.

Deep working should now mean something to you; you should be able to identify what parts of your workload will require deep work, and which parts you can do while shallow working. Try putting these differences into writing. On a piece of paper, draw out two columns. Label these Deep Work and Shallow Work. Think about all the tasks your work requires you to do, and put each task under one of these categories. Just knowing these differences and knowing when you need to use different working styles is fundamental to implementing them successfully in life.

The next step is to think about what exactly your deep-work sessions will look like. It's important to have a clear picture in your head. How do you plan to minimize distractions? How long is a deep-work session for you? Will you take breaks? What parts of your environment can you change to make them less distracting? What will you do with your phone? What happens if someone distracts you? How will you get back into the flow of deep work if a distraction does occur? It's good to be prepared and plan for these situations so you are not relying solely on emotive decisions in the moment.

The way you deep work should be kept consistent. Cal Newport even recommends having deep-working "rituals" in place. These serve to subconsciously reinforce that you are about to start deep working. Newport's own ritual looks a bit like this: He will take the same walk to work (different from his regular), go to the same office space, and make the same coffee in the same cup. These actions are purposely different to those he does when his goal is shallow work, and they help his brain seamlessly slip into deep-work mode.

What rituals can you implement to help you? Are you able to work in a different location? Are you able to drink something different? Maybe playing a certain type of music or doing breathwork before can be part of your ritual? Whatever you choose, ritualizing deep work is a fantastic way to distinguish it from other work commitments.

Planning, Protecting, and Measuring Deep Work

A key aspect of introducing more deep work into your life is planning, protecting, and measuring it. Failure to plan the times when you will deep work will, for most people, lead to the deep-work session being skipped or not fully utilized. The deep-work-to-shallow-work ratio and the deep-work philosophies (both mentioned below) are great ways to begin this planning process. Once you have planned your deep-working time, it is vital to protect it. Treat your scheduled deep-working sessions as you would a meeting or other commitment.

A great way to achieve this is by blocking that time off in your calendar. Decide when you want to start deep work and when you want to finish, and most importantly, do not allow yourself to skip it. Planning your time is making a commitment to yourself; make sure you uphold that commitment. If someone suggests a call during your deep-work time, you can't. You are busy. You have a commitment. Many people will see the time they block off for personal commitments as amendable—do not be one of those people. Respect your new deep-working habit the same way you would respect a meeting with an important client or boss.

By properly planning and protecting your deep-work sessions, you should be able to adequately measure the time spent deep working. These measurements will prove useful when assessing your own productivity and workload, as you will be able to see what ratio of quality high-focus work produces what results. If you have blocked off time in your calendar and protected that time, you can easily look back and know exactly how much deep work you were able to achieve.

This is also a good point to remind you that deep working is a skill, and like all skills, you can get better at it. Being able to focus your attention on a cognitively demanding task for long periods is difficult. If you are not used to working in this manner, then spending one hour straight on deep work might be too long. There's no shame in starting small and building a great deep-working habit over time.

The Deep-Work-to-Shallow-Work Ratio

By now you should have a clear idea of which of your tasks require deep work and which require shallow work. The next part is to work out the perfect ratio of working hours between each working method. How many hours a week should you spend on deep work? How many hours a week should you spend on shallow work? Although each job role will have a different answer, Cal Newport identifies knowing the answer to be vital to the implementation of deep work and increased productivity.

If you are employed, this will be something you figure out with your boss or manager. How long do they want you to spend replying to emails? How long do they want you to spend on project proposals? By knowing your ratio, you can identify when things aren't working for whatever reason.

For example, if your boss and you identify that the perfect ratio is 1:1, with twenty hours a week being spent on shallow work and twenty hours being spent on deep work, then a week where you are only able to achieve three hours of deep work highlights a problem. This problem could be with your workload or with the ratio, but it should open up a productive conversation with your boss or manager.

Deep-Work Philosophies

If you are self-employed or working on a passion project, Newport suggests that one of the best ways to achieve greater levels of deep working is to have a deep-working philosophy. This philosophy will be critical to your ability to implement deep work into your day-to-day life, as it will guide your scheduling decisions.

Different people in different fields will find value in different scheduling philosophies. The way a stockbroker fits deep work into his workday will likely be completely different from how a life coach does. For this reason, it's important to think realistically, not just ideally, about which would be best suited for you. The following philosophies, as outlined by Newport in his book, should serve as a good starting point.

Monastic – This philosophy's core principle is to increase deep-work time by eliminating or radically reducing shallow-work commitments. A famous example of this would be J. K. Rowling in her efforts to complete the final Harry Potter book. Rowling checked herself into a five-star hotel and made finishing the book her sole commitment; she ended up staying at the Balmoral hotel for six months! This seems like quite a radical move, but for Rowling, it was perfect for eliminating any distractions and shallow-work commitments that weren't serving her current goal.

Bimodal – As the name suggests, the bimodal philosophy involves dividing your time between two modes: deep and shallow. You will switch modes either on a weekly or monthly basis to best achieve the perfect balance needed for your goals. For example, you might choose to spend one entire month working on the code for a new app you are building, and then the following month sending emails and working on the promotional aspects of the project.

Rhythmic – This involves shifting between deep work and shallow work on a daily schedule. For example, scheduling two hours of deep work first thing every morning and then allowing the rest of the day to be occupied by shallow work.

Journalistic – This method involves opportunistically fitting in deep work whenever you can. This method would work well for those who have a constantly changing schedule. For example, if the majority of your day needs to be taken up with shallow-work tasks, you might find opportunities to have a deep-work session when a meeting gets canceled or when you unexpectedly finish your workload for the day early.

As you can see, deep work is pretty individual. Different jobs, workloads, workstyles, and personalities will benefit from different methods and attitudes to deep working. Finding your own style of deep work may take some time, and doing the cognitive "reps" to get you to sustain that focus may take even longer. But the rewards of habitual deep focus on cognitively demanding tasks have never been higher. While the convenience of mobile phones and social media continue to make sustained attention rare, there has never been a better time to take control of your focus and harness it for your own gain.

Chapter Takeaways

- Self-learners are able to proactively create their own personal development curriculum, set their own goals, and determine their own syllabus for improvement—whether that's personally or professionally.

- You need to be clear on your goals, figure out what skills are most urgently needing development, then allow the SMART acronym to help you create a roadmap for the future. Goals should be specific, measurable, achievable, meaningful, and time limited.

- Make a list of resources and be clear about your learning style and where you can access learning materials. Then, create a schedule with realistic deadlines and benchmarks to keep you on track. Roping in others can help keep you accountable. Finally, make sure you are spending some time reflecting on your process, making honest adjustments as you go.

- Deep work is focused, productive work and is a rare skill in our world of distraction. Focusing without distraction allows us to be more deeply creative and solve problems at a higher level. Deep work takes commitment and discipline. Try to clearly define what deep work looks like for you, how to fit it in, its ratio to shallow work, and how to implement it via consistent ritual and habit.

- Deep work needs to be planned for, scheduled, and protected from encroachment. Measure it and adjust accordingly. Understand the amount of deep work you're aiming for and let nothing interfere with or interrupt it.

- Your unique deep-work philosophy will depend on your personality as well as the nature of the task. Whether your approach is monastic, bimodal, rhythmic, or journalistic, take the time to figure out how best to bring more deep work into your own life and commit to it.

CHAPTER EIGHT: Passive Versus Active Learning and How to Capitalize

Active learning is much more intrinsically motivating than passive learning because it encourages active participation from the learner. Active learners are creating their own knowledge, connecting existing ideas, and testing them through experimentation, observation, and communication with peers. This creates an environment where students can learn in an exploratory way, feel prepared to exit their comfort zones, and build on their passions.

Through these conversations and activities, students are able to develop analytical thinking as well as collaboration and self-direction skills, making it a better preparation for lifelong learning. By incorporating real-world lessons into your material, you give yourself an enriching educational experience that can help create impactful life-changing events. Let's learn how you can transition to being an active learner!

Jimmy had always been a curious child. He loved learning about different cultures and yearned to explore the world beyond his small town in Nebraska. But he knew that wasn't possible; his parents were struggling just to keep food on the table, so there was no money for extravagant adventures or trips out of state. But then Jimmy's fifth grade teacher, Mrs. Johnson, introduced her students to something wonderful: role-playing games!

She explained how these games could be used as an immersive way to learn about history and other cultures from around the globe without ever leaving their classroom. Jimmy was immediately intrigued by this new form of education and jumped right into every game with enthusiasm. From pretending they were ancient Egyptians building pyramids in class to creating civilizations during Medieval Europe, each adventure transported him further away from home than he'd ever dreamed possible, all while teaching important lessons of culture and history along the way!

As time went on, Jimmy's knowledge grew exponentially through these role-play experiences with his classmates. His grades shot up too; it turned out that understanding facts wasn't enough if you didn't have a real connection or sense of context behind them! By connecting emotionally with what he learned through role-playing activities, Jimmy finally got an A+ in history class instead of another C+.

Mrs. Johnson hadn't just taught her students about historical events; she had also shown them how fun learning could be when done properly! Through those educational journeys filled with laughter and discovery, Jimmy found himself more excited than ever before for each new day at school, and he eventually discovered that knowledge is indeed power after all!

Jimmy's story is an excellent example of how active-learning strategies such as role-playing can make a significant impact on learning. Let's find out what active learning is and how you can have as much fun in the classroom as Jimmy did! Whether you are a student or an educator, everyone can benefit from incorporating these strategies into their learning routines. Let's begin!

Active learning is a type of engaged education that encourages student participation and involvement in their own educational journey. Meyers and Jones (1993) describe active learning as anything that includes "providing opportunities for students to talk and listen, read, write, and reflect as they approach course content." It helps to foster critical thinking and collaboration while providing an opportunity for students to interact with the material they are studying in a more meaningful way (Snider, Schnurer, 2002).

Studies have found that active learning can improve academic achievement (Carini et al., 2006), reduce student stress levels, and create a stronger sense of community within the classroom (Cardozo et al., 2020). By encouraging students to take an active role in their learning, students are better able to comprehend complex topics, become more confident in their abilities, and participate more willingly in group discussions or activities (Bonwell, Eison, 1991).

Additionally, it can provide teachers with insight into how well each student understands the material being presented and offer a chance for them to gauge how best to facilitate deeper learning opportunities for everyone involved. (Meyers, Jones, 1993).

Active-learning strategies are essential in modern classrooms because they promote autonomy, creativity, critical thinking, and problem-solving, and they intrinsically motivate students to continually leave their comfort zones and stretch their abilities, thus giving learners the tools they need to become successful throughout their educational career by helping them build a solid foundation from the start.

Within the classroom, active learning can take many forms, from student-centered presentations to collaborative problem-solving and discussions. Teachers who use this type of educational practice often guide students through activities that involve them in the learning process, such as having them explore a source and draw conclusions about it, holding a debate and having the students teach each other, or designing an experiment to test a hypothesis.

It's an excellent way for teachers to engage their pupils on a deeper level and encourage creative thinking and meaningful discourse (Walker, Warhurst, 2000). Here are some other examples you may have encountered: collective brainstorming, solving intriguing case studies, getting pupils to teach each other using real-world data to solve problems, creating mind maps, flipping the classroom, and gamification.

Active learning enhances communication and cognitive abilities (Harris et al., 2019). Active participation significantly improves the quality and amount of communication with the teacher and among the students not only verbally, but also through a variety of nonverbal ways. For example, you would focus more on your facial expressions, hand movements, and body posture. Non-verbal cues are a powerful tool in helping students learn and retain information.

From pointing to an image or diagram in order to explain something visually, to folding arms as a signal for students to settle down, non-verbal cues are invaluable for the classroom environment. For example, smiling or nodding when a child correctly answers a question can encourage them to take more risks and answer more confidently. You might even have observed this phenomenon in your life outside the classroom. Similarly, using gestures such as "thumbs-up" or repeating concepts in different ways can help students visualize their understanding of the material better.

After collecting research on active learning, faculty from Carnegie Mellon University's Human-Computer Interaction Institute concluded that engaging students through interactive activities, discussions, feedback, and AI-enhanced technologies led to improved academic performance compared to passive learning (traditional lectures, lessons, or readings).

Moreover, several other studies found that active learning improves student achievement. An overview study by Freeman et al. is the most compelling (2014). According to the findings of this study, students were one and a half times more likely to fail in a lecture-based class than in an active-learning class. After all this compelling evidence, I am sure you would like to know how you can benefit from active learning as well. Well, fret not! I got you!

Ten Learning Methods to Turn Passive Learning into Active Learning

Since you can't observe what goes on inside a learner's mind and see if someone is actually actively thinking hard and developing connections or if they are just passively trying to memorize what is being studied, you have to resort to active learning techniques to make sure you and your students (in case you are an educator) are employing the right learning techniques.

Finding the right personal active learning strategy can make all the difference when it comes to mastering new material. Each person needs to determine which approach works best for them; if it's more of an auditory experience, perhaps listening to lectures or audio recordings can help you better process information, whereas if it's a visual approach, try making charts and sticking notes around your workspace.

In case you prefer experiential learning, try taking part in activities related to what you're studying, such as joining a debate club if you're studying politics or joining a drama club in case you are studying literature. If you think questioning and reflecting help you understand and retain information better, try keeping a study journal and writing down your thoughts after you're done reading. Whatever you do, the key thing is ensuring there's an interactive element; don't just read or watch videos without participating in some way.

When it comes to learning, there's a big difference between *deep learning* and *surface learning*. Deep learning requires in-depth analysis and familiarizing oneself with the subject, while surface-level learning more closely resembles memorizing facts without delving into the why of them. Surface learning is the type that you've probably been doing your whole life. Scan, skim, and write down some notes. Review and study them sometimes, or not.

Deep learners learn because they desire to. They apply the knowledge to their own objectives. They are *intrinsically motivated* to learn, whether because the material is fascinating to them or because they need the knowledge for a future career. And you'll see that more often than not, they tend to apply more active-learning techniques as compared to passive ones.

Remember Jimmy? How his grades shot up and he actually started to find the content meaningful after his teacher started supplementing her lessons with role-playing games? He went from being a surface learner to a deep learner, and that changed his entire life. Now it's time to help you achieve this too!

The first step is to choose the best ways to study based on your goals and the topic you want to learn about. As mentioned earlier, not all active-learning strategies are equally effective, so you need to pay extra attention to

your study goals in order to curate the best plan of action for *you*. For example, do you need to memorize facts, boost your problem-solving skills, or increase your knowledge of a subject? Knowing your goals will point you toward learning techniques such as practice questions, role-playing, flashcards, or thought journals that are tailored to fit your needs.

Dr. John Dunlosky analyzed dozens of scholarly papers and ranked commonly used active-learning strategies from least effective to most effective. He ranked active recalling, testing and evaluating yourself, reflecting and questioning, repeated exposure, and just in time learning as the most effective active-learning strategies widely in use, whereas using mental imagery for learning, summarization, and highlighting are the least effective. To be clear, these are all superior to passively reviewing and re-reading, but there is a clear hierarchy of efficacy within active learning methods. They are as follows.

High-Retention Active Learning Methods

1. Highlighting and Annotating

Many students find that annotating their study texts with highlighter pens or writing in the margins help them concentrate and improve their learning. Simply picking what to highlight, underline, or annotate challenges you to think critically and generate your own response to the material. To apply this strategy, first quickly skim through the material to get a sense of what it's about. Then go back and read it again, pausing at the conclusion of each paragraph to identify the important ideas. You might want to annotate the page margins with brief remarks and questions or mark different types of information with different-colored pens, but be cautious not to highlight too much that it becomes obtrusive.

Then you determine what you want to emphasize or underline to assist you in identifying primary elements and their significance. You could choose to emphasize:

- a sentence or word that expresses a key idea
- quotations
- statistics
- specialized terminology
- data that is important or beneficial
- examples or links to related ideas

This technique is not intended to replace taking your own notes, but it may serve as the initial step in developing diagrammatic notes (including mind maps, also called spider diagrams or flowcharts) and preparing for essays.

For example, annotating literature books can be a great way to go beyond just reading the text. It's like digging into the book with additional information and perspectives that help you better understand its themes, messages, and symbolism. There are several approaches you can take when annotating: for starters, jot down key words, phrases, or other notable passages within the book. Additionally, make note of any unfamiliar words or concepts you come across and look up their definitions; this will help expand your vocabulary as well as enhance your comprehension of the text.

2. Reflecting and Questioning

Learners benefit from reflection because it allows them to create a personal link with the content at hand and see how it fits into a bigger picture. While annotating and highlighting a book, you can continually post questions throughout your annotations, such as "what does this mean?" or "does this represent something else?" "What if I connect this theme to the other major themes?" "How can I connect this to my own life?" "Why does this passage resonate so deeply within me?"

In doing so, you'll naturally approach the material more critically by chipping away at its surface layers in order to get to its core messages or intent. Don't forget to capture what emotions arise when reading a particular section; did any parts inspire awe, anger, or confusion? A proper annotation will help ensure that you get the most out of what you read by helping you reflect and question the material along the way.

For example, while re-reading *Jane Eyre* for like the tenth time in three years, I wrote the following passage that I recorded in my diary:

Reflecting on Jane Eyre *always brings me a feeling of warmth and understanding. It's so amazing to think that Charlotte Brontë wrote this powerful character back in 1847, and yet even today, you can still relate to so much of her journey. I truly admire how she perseveres in the face of adversity and bravely and with dignity finds her own way through life's hurdles.*

Her fierce independence, strength of character, and good moral principles are timeless qualities we all aspire to. Although she is struggling with oppressive societal constraints that feel an awful lot like today, it really speaks to how little has changed in our modern lives—something that I find both comforting yet unsettling at the same time.

You can clearly see how I have managed to reflect on the book's themes by *retrieving, elaborating, and connecting* the subject matter to my own life. Thus, exemplifying its meaning and my own understanding of it.

3. Brainstorming and Ideating

Brainstorming is an excellent method for generating a large number of ideas that you would not be able to develop by simply sitting down with a pen and paper.

Ideation, or idea generation, is a great technique to brainstorm. It is an art form that requires a skilled facilitator and an experienced team. However, we're all here to learn, and here's how you may start learning to be a good brainstorming session facilitator for yourself and others. Remember, brainstorming is about creating a secure, creative environment in which people may say anything and be crazy without fear of being judged, so that new ideas might emerge.

Begin by setting a time limit. As the facilitator, you must be intentional about scheduling time for your team to be in "brainstorm mode." During this time span, the only purpose is to generate as many ideas as possible, and judging those ideas is prohibited. The session should typically last between fifteen and sixty minutes.

Begin with a problem statement, a point of view, questions like "How might we?" and a plan or goal, and stay on topic. Brainstorming sessions, according to Alex Osborn, the originator of the technique, should always address a specific issue or problem statement (also known as a point of view), as sessions addressing several questions are inefficient. Begin with a well-stated problem or inquiry.

For example, "How is feminism portrayed in *Jane Eyre*?" "How might we translate Jane's struggle within a man-dominated society in the 1900s to modern day?" This approach has been refined by design thinkers and other ideation professionals into the art of framing problem statements through approaches. These are "how might we" inquiries, to be specific.

Defer judgment (both verbal and non-verbal) and encourage wild, crazy ideas. Don't roll your eyes in case someone within the group says something that doesn't sit well with you. The focal point of these sessions is to encourage diversity of thought, not conformity.

Therefore, keep an open mind and encourage others to do the same. Moreover, aim for quantity to generate as many ideas as possible and keep building on them instead of shunning ideas you don't agree with. Try to say "and" instead of "but" and encourage others to do the same. This simple trick takes some practice, but it works surprisingly well to keep the momentum going.

Writing down your ideas on a regular basis is an invaluable practice for any creative person. If you don't take the time to do it, there's no knowing when you might forget something great. It's easy to be busy and let the moment pass by, but if you're serious about developing your ideas, it pays to take notes regularly. It doesn't need to take long, either. Just jot down some notes and key words during your coffee break or while you're on the bus home (we get the best ideas then, don't we?). Just be sure they really are ideas that you can come back to and work on later!

4. Tracking and Game-Based Learning

A learning track is a series of activities designed to help you gain knowledge and build skills. Maintaining an accurate record of our habits is especially crucial when we are attempting to attain a goal such as improved mental or physical health, increased productivity, or mastery of a new skill. We can have a better understanding of when we are successful and the reasons that may be assisting or inhibiting our progress by recording the behaviors we are attempting to implement (or break).

This enables us to make any additional changes required to ensure success, or even to alter methods entirely. Let's assume we're trying to establish a practice of daily journaling before bed, but we're usually unsuccessful on days when we go to bed late.

This could mean that we should strive to go to bed earlier, or if that isn't an option, we should modify our objective to journaling first thing in the morning instead. You can use an app or a spreadsheet to continually log in your progress.

Games can include elements like goals, interaction, feedback, problem-solving, competition, story, and enjoyable learning environments, all of which can boost student engagement and motivation. Game-based learning entails creating learning activities with game features and game principles that are inherent in the learning activities themselves. In an economics course, for example, you can participate in a virtual stock-trading contest; in a clinical psychology course, you might role-play as a therapist engaging in a therapeutic intervention.

The incorporation of game components such as point systems, leaderboards, badges, or other game-related elements into "traditional" learning activities to boost engagement and motivation works wonderfully well.

For example, an online discussion forum for a psychology course may be gamified with a badge system, with students receiving a "Wilhelm Wundt" badge after ten postings, a "Sigmund Freud" badge after twenty postings, a "Mary Whiton Calkins " badge after thirty, an "Albert Bandura" badge after forty, and so on. Students can see the online badges that their peers have achieved in ideal gamified learning environments to create a sense of comradery or rivalry.

5. The Feynman Technique

The Feynman Technique is a great way to deepen your understanding of any subject. The key is to take complex topics and break them down into layman's terms so that you can understand them better and remember them more easily. To implement the technique, start by writing the topic at the top of a blank page.

Study it thoroughly. Then, explain it out loud as if you were teaching it to someone else, or if you have access to someone who is unfamiliar with the topic, ask if you could explain it to them. This forces you to clarify your own thinking and identify gaps in your knowledge. Once you're done talking, summarize what you just said onto the page. If there are any areas where your explanation wasn't clear, go back and try again, repeating the process until everything makes sense!

6. Discussing and Peer Reviewing

Peer review and discussions, such as reviewing written work, finding misconceptions or missing knowledge, summarizing, and providing feedback, are cognitively demanding activities, all of which aid in the consolidation and deepening of knowledge and understanding. Whether in the classroom setting or a professional work environment, crafting your ideas in an interactive way that is open to criticism is sure to make them stronger. Begin by analyzing your own opinion alongside others with different perspectives.

Collaborate and discuss with your peers, as it can reveal overlooked angles you may have missed during solitary creative brainstorming.

An example of peer reviewing might involve two students in a classroom setting reading, editing, and improving the grammar, word choice, and organization of one another's essays. This collaboration gives them more insight into the writing process and teaches them to think critically about their own ideas as well as take into account other perspectives.

Having other people comment on your input is invaluable, as it allows you to present unique arguments and refine them when constructive criticism is provided. The best way to practice discussing and peer reviewing is by creating small groups or having one-on-one conversations. Setting up a discussion board with different topics that can be debated is also a great way to practice articulating your thoughts in an organized manner.

Peer review promotes active learning by including students in the feedback process as opposed to simply obtaining comments passively from teachers. You can also join an online community of others who are interested in the same topic and receive support, accountability, assistance, and other benefits.

7. Hiring A Coach and Deliberate Practicing

Having a learning coach can be immensely beneficial to your academic journey. They have the skills and expertise to help you stay organized, create effective study plans, and set achievable goals for yourself. A learning coach can help balance schoolwork with other commitments like extracurricular activities or after-school jobs, as well as encourage positive healthy habits that are conducive to better learning outcomes.

Good learning coaches also provide students with timely and constructive feedback on their assignments to maintain focus and improve their performance. An experienced coach is invaluable in fostering an environment of success while keeping you motivated during challenging times at school.

Coaches also have the unique capacity to help turn traditional practice into meaningful, deliberate practice. Deliberate practice involves *breaking a skill down into smaller parts and homing in on each section until it's mastered.* Coaches are able to do this because they possess knowledge related to improving and mastering craftsmanship, be it athletics or any other field, that the average person may not have.

For example, a coach may recognize that a shooter isn't following through during her practice shots and adjust her technique accordingly to improve accuracy. Ultimately, relying on coaches while learning anything can be very beneficial in making optimal progress toward mastery.

8. Experiential Learning

Experiential learning is all about getting hands-on experience. It's about diving into the experience rather than just reading or listening to lectures about it, which allows us to interact with the material and really understand it in a deeper way. This type of learning helps us retain information more easily, encourages active participation and problem-solving, develops critical thinking skills, and allows us to gain an understanding of how our actions affect others.

Experiential learning can take many different forms, from organized classroom activities, hands-on language immersion, educational field trips, participation in professional organizations, and real-world simulations, to internships and self-directed projects outside of the classroom. Whatever form we choose for experiential learning, it's definitely worth the effort.

So the next time you hear your teacher tell you that your overall grade will now include an internship, rejoice! Such experience will help you grow and develop in ways traditional lectures just can't match! I remember my own psychology internships, and in some ways, they taught me more than I ever learned sitting in that classroom.

9. Repeated Exposure and Just in Time Learning

Repeated exposure is a great way to learn something new. It involves taking the time to interact with a piece of information over and over until it has been internalized. This technique can be used to teach almost anything, from language-speaking skills to math concepts to even facts related to history. The possibilities are endless.

Repeated exposure helps build understanding and confidence in any task because learners are forced to dwell on content until it clicks. The key is pacing one's learning: going slow and steady, always returning to any material if necessary. Though repetition can often seem tedious, sticking with a subject while monitoring progress leads to success!

You can make use of flashcards and concept maps to help you easily access the material you are planning to learn. I do something really weird and am made fun of by my friends all the time. What I do is that if I want to remember something (be it a concept I am learning, a quote from a favorite movie, or positive affirmations, I always write them down on a brightly colored sticky note and stick it to my mirror. Therefore, every morning when I get ready, I automatically glance at them, and believe me, I still remember my grocery list from five years ago!

Just in time learning is a great way to keep up with ever-evolving trends, concepts, and just life in general. This type of learning emphasizes acquiring skills as you need them, allowing you to stay on top of your field's trends and nuances. Rather than investing countless hours into outdated material, your focus is put on making sure learners have the necessary information for their *current role*. This method caters perfectly to any individual looking for ways to stay ahead in their profession without sacrificing all their extra time.

What you should do is archive all information based on priority. Any huge chunks of information that you do not immediately need can be saved for later. This way you will only need to know what is absolutely required within that moment alone. Our brains can only take up a certain amount of information within a specified period of time, so learning everything all together at once will be useless anyway.

10. Active Recalling, Testing and Evaluating Yourself

Before diving into spaced repetition systems, it's necessary to understand how our brains work. In order for us to retain any information in our brain, we must refresh it at regular intervals. Let's imagine you hear that "Madrid is the capital of Spain." If you don't use that information, you'll probably forget about it once you finish reading this article or later. However, if you continue to "learn" that Madrid is the capital of Spain" through text or explanation, you will remember it better.

The point is this:

The more frequently you see specific pieces of information, the less frequently you will need to replenish your recollection of it.

Active recall is a technique for memorizing a topic that involves transferring information from short-term memory to long-term memory. The spaced repetition system (SRS) is the best method for practicing it. One way you can practice active recalling and spaced repetition is by using flashcards. Making flashcards is a great way to sharpen your learning skills! It's an especially helpful tool for memorizing vocabulary, concepts, and formulas. To get started, all you need is some blank index cards and something to write with.

Begin by dividing the card into two sections: writing the term on one side of the card and its definition or explanation on the other side. Use colors to separate words from definitions, or maybe even draw a simple illustration that will help you remember it better! Flashcard studying is always more fun if you make them creative and colorful! Finally, challenge yourself with how many cards you can remember each day, then add more as needed for more difficult concepts.

Making flashcards is an awesome way to spruce up your learning skills and make memorization easier, so go get creative! It helps you remember the solution to a question, and when you use it consistently enough, your brain recognizes it as essential information. The information is then stored in your long-term memory, where you can easily recall it.

Self-learning can be challenging because it's hard to gauge how much you know or don't know. Therefore, **it is really important to test and evaluate yourself along the way**. From checking for comprehension after a lesson to reflecting on how far you've come in the learning process, there are lots of ways to monitor your progress and give yourself a pat on the back.

One way is to practice oral exams with a friend—use them as an examiner and take turns answering questions you create together! This method provides accountability and helps you remember key information.

Of course, there's nothing better than a good old-fashioned test or light quiz to fully gauge your understanding of the material. If you choose this option, be sure to shake things up; multiple choice, true/false, and matching are all great options! Evaluating yourself can feel intimidating at first, but it doesn't have to be. Utilize creative approaches combined with traditional methods and allow yourself grace along the journey. You may surprise yourself at what you know!

Chapter Takeaways

- According to Dr. John Dunlosky, the most effective active learning strategies are: active recalling, testing and evaluating yourself, reflecting and questioning, repeated exposure, and just in time learning.
- Each person needs to determine which approach works best for them based on their preferred method of processing information. In order to learn effectively, it is important to participate in an activity related to what you are trying to learn about rather than passively consuming information.
- Many students find that annotating their study materials with highlighter pens or writing in the margins boosts their concentration and learning. You can approach the material critically by reflecting and questioning. Ask yourself: did any parts inspire awe, anger, or confusion? You can also generate a large number of ideas by brainstorming and ideating; they can aid you in generating a large number of ideas in a short amount of time.
- Try incorporating game aspects such as point systems, leaderboards, badges, or other game-

related elements into "conventional" learning exercises to increase engagement and motivation. Discuss and participate in peer reviews to receive some constructive feedback. You can also hire an expert or a coach to help you break down your learning goals into sizable digestible chunks. Get some hands-on experience (experiential learning) to solidify those concepts.

- Take ample breaks in between learning sessions and take your time in learning new concepts. Repetition is key, and you have to consistently interact with information until perfectly understood. Active recall is a technique for memorizing that involves transferring information from short-term memory to long-term memory; using flashcards is one approach to practice active recall and spaced repetition. Keep on testing yourself to make sure you understand the information.

CHAPTER NINE: Gamification—For Learning, Retention, and Motivation

Gamification is an increasingly popular active learning strategy that can liven up any educational environment. By providing rewards and challenges, gamification keeps you engaged and motivated to learn while enlivening the atmosphere. This fun approach is based on theories of motivation, cognitive psychology, and behavioral science and promotes cooperative problem-solving alongside competition.

Gamification has been gaining traction in recent years as a way to boost motivation and productivity. By incorporating elements such a game-like challenges and rewards into the environment, you are more likely to stay engaged in day-to-day tasks. However, it's important not to forget the importance of intrinsic motivation and passion; if those factors aren't present, the initial motivating factors provided by gamification will have little long-term success.

Creating an environment where people feel free to pursue their interests can foster meaningful relationships that go beyond simple challenge-based reward systems. If a strong sense of purpose exists, you are more likely to stay motivated over long periods of time, regardless of gamified elements. Let's see how you can make studying for that exam just a little bit more fun!

The world of video games was a place of total escapism for Michael. As soon as he booted up his computer and clicked on the game, he felt like he had been transported to another realm entirely. Every detail in the game seemed incredibly lifelike, from the characters' facial expressions to the sound effects that made it seem like he was really there.

Michael found himself quickly immersed in this alternate universe where danger lurked around every corner but also possibilities were endless. He learned how to survive through trial and error; if something didn't work out exactly as planned, he simply tried again until it did work out perfectly. This process taught him invaluable lessons about problem-solving skills and perseverance, qualities that would serve him well in real life too!

But more than anything else, what kept Michael coming back to this virtual reality was its sheer entertainment value: Whenever things got dull or stressful at home or school or work, playing these games allowed him to take a break from reality while still engaging with an exciting storyline full of puzzles and plot twists.

It provided just enough distraction without completely disconnecting him from reality; instead of vegging out on the couch, watching TV all night long (which often left him feeling even more drained), spending time gaming gave Michael a sense of accomplishment when all was said and done because not only did he feel entertained but also smarter after each session!

At times, it almost felt surreal; here Michael was learning valuable lessons while simultaneously being taken away into another realm—one filled with dragons and knights and castles but one that could actually teach us so much about ourselves too! Gaming isn't just a way for people to escape their worries, but rather an avenue for them to learn new skill sets whilst having fun along the way—something no other medium can quite provide!

Judging from Michael's experience with video games, we can deduce that video games can be used as essential tools to improve learning, retention, and motivation. You might be wondering why on earth I am talking about learning and *video games* within the same sentence. Because surely not! They are nothing more than a frivolous pastime! You're right, and I am sure my mom would agree with this sentiment, but I, however, am here to explain just how beneficial incorporating in-game elements such as goals, rules, problem-solving, feedback, and fun can help educators and learners master concepts that might otherwise be really challenging to learn on their own. So, what exactly is gamification and why has game-based learning been such a hot buzz within the learning community?

Gamification has become increasingly popular in recent years as an approach to learning and teaching. Essentially, it is the use of game elements and digital game-based strategies to engage students or learners to have more fun while optimizing their learning, motivation, engagement, retention, and performance. These elements include leaderboards, rewards, online badges, and many other elements that are designed to help users or students stay engaged.

Traditional methods of passive learning can be enhanced creatively by incorporating gamification elements, such as online challenges that students must work together to solve (Bukley, Doyle, 2014). Ultimately, these fun approaches motivate learners to engage with course materials more deeply and effectively, providing deeper understanding and retention through an enjoyable process (Barata, 2013).

It has been demonstrated that playing video games during training can enhance cognitive performance (Green, Bavelier, 2003). The use of game elements in education may enhance how well the brain processes new information and recalls it. The general features of gamified lectures, such as the audio-visual presentation, little chunks of schematized information, brief time gaps, and frequently recurring patterns, may help with this. Any new data we gain is lost unless it somehow makes its way into our long-term memory, and gamification provides the structure needed for this to happen.

By giving us an organized structure of rules, levels, and rewards, our brains are able to easily access its two processing channels (visual and auditory) to effectively store information in our long-term memory by integrating it within our existing schemas in a creative way that makes for easier recall. So whether we're trying to remember vocabulary words or absorb scientific concepts, gamification can make it easier than ever before!

Dopamine, or the feel-good hormone, is released whenever we are rewarded for a specific action. Gamification focuses on giving learners instantaneous feedback that might not otherwise be available. By giving virtual rewards for achieving learning goals, learners begin to associate the learning with positive emotions, prompting them to try to repeat it (i.e., seek out more learning). Video gaming, more specifically a tank simulation, has been linked to endogenous dopamine release in the ventral striatum (VS), according to a study by Koepp et al., 1998). The VS is a component of the dopaminergic pathways and is linked to motivation and reward processing (Knutson, Greer, 2008)

Moreover, a study of organizational behavior students' perspectives looked at how involvement in a gamified course motivated students in general and looked at the individual effect of certain game aspects. Sixty-seven point seven percent of participants said the gamified course was more or significantly more motivating than a standard course (Chapman, 2018). Gabe Zicherman, author of *Gamification by Design*, conducted research that demonstrates that gamification can be used to make activities not just more fun but also more productive.
Essential Elements of Gamification and How to Apply Them to Your Own Learning Routines

Now that we have established the importance of gamification in learning, let's move on to the components of gamification, namely goals, rules, problem-solving, feedback, and fun. We will now explore how to incorporate each of these into your personal study routines.

Goals and Rewards

Lucy was a bright student, but she had always struggled with astronomy. She simply couldn't remember all the facts and figures needed to pass her upcoming exam. Her professor recommended her to try something called "gamification," using game principles like goals, quests, and puzzles in order to learn better.

At first Lucy thought it sounded silly, but she decided to give it a shot. She created a quest for herself: master the entire course by studying for three hours each day until the exam date. She began by addressing her current level of understanding (which would be her starting point) and identified her end point (due date of the exam).

To make things easier, she mapped out the entire chunk of time she had available between her starting and end points. She called them "path markers." Her markers consisted of reading her textbook, attempting assignments, and doing puzzles and quizzes.

To motivate herself further, she set up rewards; if she completed her daily tasks on time, then she would get small treats like candy or an extra hour of sleep over the weekend. Lucy started off by breaking down every topic into smaller chunks that were easier for her to understand and memorize. Instead of just reading textbooks from start to finish, Lucy made sure to make use of different kinds of learning materials, such as online videos or interactive quizzes, so that each session stayed interesting for her too!

The more Lucy used gamification techniques in order to study, the more confident and motivated she felt about passing her exam with flying colors! Every morning when Lucy woke up filled with enthusiasm at what new knowledge awaited her during today's lesson. There was no stopping this determined girl! When she reached her end point, she passed the exam with flying colors and went out to celebrate her success under the stars with everyone she held dear.

When we think of quests and tasks in games, we often associate them with getting a new high score or beating a boss. However, these same concepts can be applied to something like studying for an exam, just like Lucy applied them. Think of your desired grade as the ultimate reward that you have to climb through levels of studying, difficult problems, and other obstacles to achieve.

Small rewards along the way help fuel motivation, and reaching your goal is just as attained through hard work, patience, and understanding of material as it is in a video game. That's why setting goals in school can be looked at similarly to tasks or quests in games; you're still playing the exam-grade game. Don't forget to celebrate once all is done and dusted!

Rules

As Lucy continued along her quest to the due day of her exam, she had to make sure that she established strict rules and regulations similar to those that ruled her in-game world when she played World of Warcraft. This is important because it let her know exactly what she was allowed to do and what she wasn't.

One of the most significant aspects of video games are the rules, which govern not only how the virtual world works but also how to win the game. They not only contain explicitly defined rules but also have an evaluation of the players' efforts. Sometimes we do need to standardize our lives as such in order to achieve a goal. These rules will help us stay on the path and not stray (regardless of how much we want to binge all the new movies coming to Netflix this holiday season!).

For example, you have this huge exam coming up and you really need to get started right away. You have diligently planned your quest (the exam, similar to how Lucy planned out hers). But now you need to add the rules that are going to govern your life. A potential rule for your quest could be something as simple as "not sleeping for more than eight hours a day" and "no unnecessary travel until you have achieved all your desired goals." Perhaps the quest will only allow you to hang out with your friends for a set amount of time and only on specific days.

Remember, the quest is long and the journey arduous. There are going to be creatures and beings (Netflix, TV, Consoles, friends who always want to party) trying to stop you from making any progress and making you repeat checkpoints and distracting you from your final mission.

Here, you can work on starting to improve your concentration, dedication, and agility stats to defeat these foes. Silence that phone, unsubscribe from Netflix, turn off that TV, communicate with your friends and let them know that this is something really important to you and that you need some time to accomplish this. Remember, you have to follow the rules at all costs! Otherwise, you will be right back where you started and it'll essentially be GAME OVER!

Problem-Solving

The rules of video games may seem unrelated to real life, but they actually have some very useful educational value. For example, if you've ever played RPG games like the Legend of Zelda, you'll know that the best way to defeat challenges and progress in the game is by *carefully weighing your options and strategizing each move*. This teaches valuable lessons in problem-solving and planning that can be applied to any real-life situation.

Begin by viewing yourself as a survivor tackling tasks, solving puzzles, opening doors to secret lairs, and finding goals, a skill that can be taken into other realms, such as college or work. Every time you advance in the game, you feel accomplished and eager to take on the next challenge. Before you can employ gamification, you must recognize the issues (for example, having a close friend's wedding right before your exams) that are currently limiting you and frame them as challenges or puzzles that must be solved.

As you design the game, the primary impediment to achieving your goal (an A grade) becomes the challenge as you try to discover a way around it to go on to the "next level." You will frequently learn more information if you continue to ask questions regarding the current issue (solve puzzles, participate in dialogue choices with your friends). You might discover, for instance, that you procrastinate a lot, which has led to a lackluster situation, and that if you actually just learn to manage your time better (checkpoint), you might be able to overcome this issue.

As tackling main quests and side quests within in-game worlds often require rigorous problem-solving skills, you can apply the same skills to your real-life quest as well. With every quest you plan, your path is drastically going to change. Depending on the landscape (your subject) and the weather (level of your course), your way forward could range from a lush green shaded path in the middle of a beautiful forest, lined with flowers and fruits and fresh water all around (level of the course material: easy), to a jagged path across rocky black mountains with danger lurking around every turn (level of course material: hard).

Once you have chosen your path, you will begin your journey. The energy you decide to take on this quest is entirely up to you. You can run, sprint, skip energetically (use flashcards, quizzes, puzzles, and other interactive supplementary materials), or you can jog (practice on case studies) along the pathway leading up to your quest.

Sometimes you will need to pause and ask an NPC (non-player character within the game world; course peer in your real life) for directions. You will also frequently run into trouble with the material (unclear, missed questions, not enough illustrative examples, etc.). These impasses will hinder your progress and prevent you from moving toward your quest.

This signals a time to pause, take a deep breath, and take inventory (in the game: check your map, your health bar, your bag Make sure you have everything you need. If not, you can also use the things/ingredients you have to make your own customized weapon/dress/food/medicine; in real life: go through your course materials, check your textbook [map] and your teacher [compass]).

This is to make sure that you are on the right path and are not wandering about aimlessly. You can also team up with a local villager (an academic coach, tutor) who is familiar with the terrain you are trying to conquer. They will be able to guide you and help you figure out your next best strategy in case you get stuck high up somewhere in the misty mountains (the mountain of course materials waiting on your coffee table to come conquer them).

Feedback and Fun

Start using points, leaderboards, badges, and awards for positive feedback. For completing little but significant tasks that help you reach your larger objective, points may be given. Badges are an excellent approach to provide yourself with immediate feedback. Once you finish an assignment successfully, choose a badge that reflects your acquired expertise. While gathering feedback, don't forget to have some fun along the way! Below is an example that will further illustrate this concept.

The fog creeps in from the mountaintops as if it is calling out to you (time to take out your books and study). You have heard stories of a powerful monster that lives high up in the misty mountains, and now you are determined to find it and defeat it (that one concept you have been avoiding for a while).

You began your journey with nothing but courage and a few meager provisions (just what you need to survive—your water bottle and a few snacks should suffice. No need to bring your phone with you), yet somehow, that feels enough. As the hours go on, you find yourself trekking higher and higher into the mountainside (preparing to tackle that difficult concept). Nothing seems familiar anymore; everywhere around you is an eerie fog that refuses to lift (confusion, self-doubt).

Finally you find a campsite and try to settle down for the night (preparing to study). You glance around the campsite and notice it littered with small twigs. You get up, grab your satchel, and pick up the fallen leaves and twigs (rewards/badges; pencil and paper), small branches (textbooks), and some wild blueberries you find a bush of (lecture notes). Now you start to feel slightly cozier.

After weeks of travel through treacherous terrain and relentless rainstorms, there it is: the monster's cave (the day of the quest; the final battle also known as the day of your exam lurking dangerously close by with this being your mock exam)! You steel yourself for battle as you step inside, your heart beating faster than ever before as anticipation overwhelms your senses.

You run right back outside, not yet ready to face the monster (exam within). You return to camp to evaluate your options. You haven't really prepared all that well (only read the textbook), and now you need to re-strategize. You go back to sharpen your sword (starting to apply and connect concepts). Feeling confident the next day, you go back to fight the monster once more, but alas! Your fear gets the best of you, as you are not as readily prepared as you had imagined.

As a last resort, you turn to a local guide for help (your professor), and he helps you navigate the uncharted waters (concepts you failed to fully understand). The very next day, you grab your supplies and move toward the monster cave (the final exam) with purpose. But what lies ahead is unlike anything you could have imagined: a vast chamber filled with golden treasures (the mock exam looks mighty safe now that you are fully prepared)!

Oh, how tempting they are ... but no sooner do these thoughts cross your mind when suddenly—BAM!—something heavy hits the wall behind you! It seems like time stands still as two eyes pierce through the darkness at one end of the cavern—it is THE MONSTER (the exam)!

But as you gear up (pencil drawn, eraser held), suddenly all of your doubts evaporate into thin air. Your adrenaline spikes sky high and instinct takes over: You draw out your sword (pencil and paper) just in time to block its attack . . . the clang of metal reverberating throughout the chamber (you brilliantly tackled the first question)!

Sparks flew across both weapons as your blades meet again and again . . . It isn't long before sweat starts to drip down from every pore on your body . . . Yet somehow despite everything going against you—YOU WIN! Ancient artifacts scatter about its lair, shimmering brightly once more, not only signaling success over this formidable enemy but also marking a new chapter in life for YOU: Victory is yours!

Winning the battle feels wonderful (a shiny new badge; monster/exam slayer)! When we achieve a goal, the brain releases the neurotransmitter dopamine, a hormone associated with pleasure, which keeps us interested and prolongs playtime. That rush of dopamine is what propels and encourages us to take on the challenges ahead.

Okay, this turned out to be way more dramatic than I originally thought it would be, but what's life without a little dramatic flair? But you see how through trial and error, you received positive and negative feedback, made measured improvements, and continued to try to slay the monster. The importance of feedback in the learning process cannot be overstated. It tells us whether we are traveling in the right or wrong way, ultimately improving our strategy. You can use this example to make your own fun monster-slaying adventures too!

Chapter Takeaways

- Gamification has become increasingly popular as it is proven to be an effective approach to learning by enhancing motivation, engagement, retention, and performance. By incorporating game elements into lectures, students are motivated to engage with course materials more deeply and understand/retain information better.
- Gamification uses game principles like goals and quests to help people learn better. For example, you can create a quest for yourself to master a course by studying three hours each day until the exam date.
- To make things easier, you can map out the entire chunk of time you have available between your starting and end points, and break down every topic into smaller chunks. You can set up rewards for yourself if you complete your daily tasks on time. The more you use gamification techniques in order to

study, the more confident and motivated you will feel about passing your exam.
- When we think of quests in games, we often associate them with getting a new high score or beating a boss, but these concepts can be applied to something like studying for an exam too. Rules in video games teach valuable lessons in problem-solving and planning that can be applied to any real-life situation.
- Begin by viewing yourself as a survivor tackling tasks, solving puzzles, opening doors to secret lairs, and finding goals. As you gamify your situation, the primary impediment to achieving your goal becomes the challenge as you try to discover a way around it to go on.
- Points, leaderboards, badges, and awards can be used for positive feedback. For completing little but significant tasks that help you reach your larger objective, points may be given. Badges are an excellent approach to provide yourself with immediate feedback.

Summary Guide

CHAPTER ONE: FROM "COMFORT ZONE" TO "GROWTH ZONE"

- Embracing the uncharted terrain of leaving your comfort zones aids in the development of confidence and resilience, allowing you to continue developing and learning for the rest of your life. This acquired understanding eventually means that your comfort zone has increased even further and you are now in the growth zone.
- Psychologist Andy Molinsky has dedicated his career to understanding why people resist leaving their comfort zones, and how they can overcome that resistance using three Cs: conviction, customization, and clarity. You must develop strong convictions, which are your core beliefs, such as altruism, generosity, gratitude, integrity, accountability, and perseverance.
- Customization relates to your ability to successfully adjust your behavior to your surroundings without losing yourself in the process. Consider it "fitting in" without fully "giving in." You're still you, just slightly altered (e.g., wearing your power suit, carrying your lucky charm, etc.) to trick yourself into feeling at ease and easily

blending into your surroundings. Lastly, you must have clarity, which is obtaining an objective, rational perspective on the problems you are facing. By challenging your negative thoughts, you can gain a clearer picture of your challenges.

- Leaving your comfort zone and facing new challenges will sometimes guarantee failure. However, it is important to remember that every failure is an opportunity for us to learn and grow. Therefore, define failure as a discrepancy to help reframe your mindset. Start by looking at it as a discrepancy between your expectations and reality. Determine if the threat is real or imagined by evaluating your body's physical response.
- Additionally, create promotion goals rather than prevention goals to stay focused on what's important. This development of a goal-oriented growth mindset toward learning not only prepares you for success in your chosen profession, but it also promotes healthy personal development. Expect a good outcome but do not become attached to it, so you can enjoy the journey. Have faith in the outcome, but don't put your entire happiness on the line.

CHAPTER TWO: PASSION AND MOTIVATION FOR LIFELONG PURSUITS

- Intrinsic motivation is essential for lifelong learning and fuels the desire to keep learning new things, even if it's outside your comfort zone. This innate internal drive is what fuels your passion. Passion itself is a positive energy that you can experience in multiple areas of your life. The most common interpretation of passion in organizational studies is teleological, implying a powerful, purposive motivation to achieve an end goal.
- Intrinsic motivation comes from within and is when you do something because you want to, not because you have to. You're driven by a personal interest or enjoyment in the task itself. For example, learning to bake simply because you enjoy it.
- There are three fundamental psychological requirements identified by the self-determination theory (SDT) that are "foundational to all human beings and our ability to flourish. These requirements, which must be met for engaged, passionate people to do excellent work in any field, are autonomy (the capacity of a person to pursue their own values and interests), competence (the need to believe you are capable of reaching desired results), and relatedness (a sense of connection with others).
- To increase intrinsic motivation, it is first important to build supportive environments that encourage these things. It's important to create an environment that fosters trust and encourages healthy discourse. Second, focus

on learning goals rather than results-based goals. Learning happens regardless of whether you achieve your desired results. Lastly, connect work with a higher cause or something that gives your work greater meaning.
- Intrinsic motivation contributes to success by enabling you to build your passions and ambitions based on you rather than extraneous influences. To ignite intrinsic motivation, consider what angers or moves you emotionally, what piques your curiosity, or what you loved doing in childhood. Work on your perspective and find the one sentence that perfectly defines you.
- Take inventory of your talents and look for things that bring you joy. If something annoys or makes you feel envious, there may be an unmet desire buried there that could be worth pursuing as a passion project.

CHAPTER THREE: USING WOOP TO SET AND ACHIEVE YOUR GOALS

- WOOP (Wish, Outcome, Obstacle, and Plan) is an evidence-based intervention that guides you through an investigation of hurdles and barriers while introducing you to goal-setting. This evidence-based approach is great because it allows individuals to create a plan that addresses any difficulties they may face while also considering their desired outcome. Practicing the WOOP method helps to build confidence, increase motivation, and foster a sense of self-efficacy, which can be beneficial when striving to attain personal goals.

- First, identify your wish or goal in detail, being clear about how you know when you've achieved it. Consider something in your life that you wish to improve: your career, education, relationships, or anything else. It should be challenging, realistic, and achievable.

- Next, flesh out this outcome in your mind's eye, visualizing both the good and bad aspects. Visualizing your outcome helps you understand why you want to accomplish this specific goal. Specificity here is important because you won't be nearly as motivated to carry out your ideas if you have a hazy sense of what success would feel like or how your life would improve.

- Carefully consider the obstacles in this plan, being honest and realistic about the unavoidable effort and challenge involved. Consider what it might look and feel like to have your objective met. Spend some time thoroughly imagining, seeing, and feeling what it would be like to achieve the finest potential outcome.

- Finally, make a plan that addresses these obstacles so you'll know what to do when setbacks occur. This is important because keeping your options open will help you get up when things don't go your way.

CHAPTER FOUR: SELF-EDUCATION BEGINS AND ENDS WITH QUESTIONS

- It is important to ask the right questions when learning something new, especially if you want to learn it effectively. Empowering questions that are solution-oriented and begin with "how" will help you get started on the right foot. You should also avoid disempowering questions that focus on the negative aspects of a situation and begin with "why."
- Bloom's taxonomy offers a framework to define and classify the levels of human cognition, from basic to more in-depth thought processing. With self-learning, it is important to know how to self-question based on the following six categories: remembering, understanding, applying, analyzing, evaluating, and creating.
- Remembering knowledge: This stage concentrates on retrieving information from memory that has been obtained through instruction and experience. To do this

effectively, try using mnemonics or other memorization techniques.
- Understanding: The second stage of knowledge is all about understanding the material rather than just memorizing it. Try discussing ideas within the material with others or forming connections between that material and related topics.
- Application: The third stage of application is about taking what you have learned and being able to use it in a practical sense outside of lecture settings, such as solving math problems or creating detailed essays/plans.
- Analyzing: The fourth stage of analysis consists of taking the knowledge gained from prior stages and using it to create something original, like writing a story or designing an experiment.
- Everyone has a passion for something, but it is a challenge to take that passion and turn it into a highly coveted skill. To fight this, CaFE suggests compressing the most essential 20 percent of information into a cheat sheet. Consider four factors when creating your personal learning schedule: study duration, time of day, weekday, and frequency. Encoding is the last component of Tim's rapid skill acquisition toolset and requires you to connect new information to prior knowledge.

CHAPTER FIVE: THE SACRED, LIFE-CHANGING HABIT OF READING

- Reading is simply one of the best daily habits to cultivate no matter what your personal development goals are. Reading broadens your horizons, challenges fixed perspectives, deepens your knowledge base, and strengthens your intelligence, comprehension, critical thinking, and empathy . . . not to mention it's fun!
- Squeeze in reading where you can, but make a schedule, too, that fits your unique needs. Try different formats (such as eBooks or audiobooks) and remember to keep organized by making lists of your reading goals and making notes about the material you've read.
- Technology can be friend or foe when it comes to reading, so pay attention to whether the internet/devices are serving your reading goals or getting in the way. Be extra mindful of social media apps, as they can really distract you from your reading tasks.
- You can develop your own reading routine over time. The first step is to sit down and start developing concrete lists of what you aim to accomplish with your new reading habit. Making a physical list, whether by hand on a piece of paper or on a word processing document, is a fantastic brain workout in and of itself. It gets you thinking, and as your list grows, it becomes even another thing to read.

- Always be mindful of how much literary "junk info" you are consuming. If you put too much irrelevant junk into your brain, you're gonna get junk in return. A good strategy is to continuously take notes while you are reading and visit bookstores to find exactly what you need and limit confusion.

CHAPTER SIX: PERSONAL KNOWLEDGE MANAGEMENT AND THE LEARNING PROCESS

- Personal knowledge management (PKM) is a set of processes that a person uses in their daily activities to collect, categorize, store, search for, retrieve, and share knowledge.
- Creating a "capture habit" is the first step in personal knowledge management, which is important for lifelong learning and freedom. A capture habit involves quickly saving any helpful or inspiring information or ideas that are come across. This can be done by setting up Google Alerts, subscribing to RSS feeds, following social media accounts, etc.
- Once information is gathered, it needs to be properly labeled and organized using a system that makes sense for the task at hand. This will make it easier to find later on when needed. The goal is to make your life easier by understanding and implementing the techniques learned from gathering this information.

- The Zettelkasten method is a notetaking system developed by German sociologist Niklas Luhmann that helps you capture ideas and connect them with one another. It has three essential elements: slips of paper, a filing system, and a mind map. The slips of paper are used to record ideas, thoughts, and information, which are then sorted into different categories and filed accordingly.
- The mind map is used to visualize the relationships between different ideas. In order to make connections between concepts, you can use special strategies like bridge notes or progressive summarization. Bridge notes can be used to connect ideas, index notes to organize ideas, and topic notes to group relevant information or notes together.

CHAPTER SEVEN: CREATE YOUR OWN PERSONAL SYLLABUS AND REFLECTIVE LEARNING

- Self-learners are able to proactively create their own personal development curriculum, set their own goals, and determine their own syllabus for improvement—whether that's personally or professionally.

- You need to be clear on your goals, figure out what skills are most urgently needing development, then allow the SMART acronym to help you create a roadmap for the future. Goals should be specific, measurable, achievable, meaningful, and time limited.

- Make a list of resources and be clear about your learning style and where you can access learning materials. Then, create a schedule with realistic deadlines and benchmarks to keep you on track. Roping in others can help keep you accountable. Finally, make sure you are spending some time reflecting on your process, making honest adjustments as you go.

- Deep work is focused, productive work and is a rare skill in our world of distraction. Focusing without distraction allows us to be more deeply creative and solve problems at a higher level. Deep work takes commitment and discipline. Try to clearly define what deep work looks like for you, how to fit it in, its ratio to shallow work, and how to implement it via consistent ritual and habit.

- Deep work needs to be planned for, scheduled, and protected from encroachment. Measure it and adjust accordingly. Understand the amount of deep work you're aiming for and let nothing interfere with or interrupt it.

- Your unique deep-work philosophy will depend on your personality as well as the nature of the task. Whether your approach is monastic, bimodal, rhythmic, or journalistic, take the time to figure out how best to bring more deep work into your own life and commit to it.

CHAPTER EIGHT: PASSIVE VERSUS ACTIVE LEARNING AND HOW TO CAPITALIZE

- According to Dr. John Dunlosky, the most effective active learning strategies are: active recalling, testing and evaluating yourself, reflecting and questioning, repeated exposure, and just in time learning.
- Each person needs to determine which approach works best for them based on their preferred method of processing information. In order to learn effectively, it is important to participate in an activity related to what you are trying to learn about rather than passively consuming information.
- Many students find that annotating their study materials with highlighter pens or writing in the margins boosts their concentration and learning. You can approach the material critically by reflecting and questioning. Ask yourself: did any parts inspire awe, anger, or confusion? You can also generate a large number of ideas by brainstorming and ideating; they can aid you in generating a large number of ideas in a short amount of time.

- Try incorporating game aspects such as point systems, leaderboards, badges, or other game-related elements into "conventional" learning exercises to increase engagement and motivation. Discuss and participate in peer reviews to receive some constructive feedback. You can also hire an expert or a coach to help you break down your learning goals into sizable digestible chunks. Get some hands-on experience (experiential learning) to solidify those concepts.
- Take ample breaks in between learning sessions and take your time in learning new concepts. Repetition is key, and you have to consistently interact with information until perfectly understood. Active recall is a technique for memorizing that involves transferring information from short-term memory to long-term memory; using flashcards is one approach to practice active recall and spaced repetition. Keep on testing yourself to make sure you understand the information.

CHAPTER NINE: GAMIFICATION—FOR LEARNING, RETENTION, AND MOTIVATION

- Gamification has become increasingly popular as it is proven to be an effective approach to learning by enhancing motivation, engagement, retention, and performance. By

incorporating game elements into lectures, students are motivated to engage with course materials more deeply and understand/retain information better.
- Gamification uses game principles like goals and quests to help people learn better. For example, you can create a quest for yourself to master a course by studying three hours each day until the exam date.
- To make things easier, you can map out the entire chunk of time you have available between your starting and end points, and break down every topic into smaller chunks. You can set up rewards for yourself if you complete your daily tasks on time. The more you use gamification techniques in order to study, the more confident and motivated you will feel about passing your exam.
- When we think of quests in games, we often associate them with getting a new high score or beating a boss, but these concepts can be applied to something like studying for an exam too. Rules in video games teach valuable lessons in problem-solving and planning that can be applied to any real-life situation.
- Begin by viewing yourself as a survivor tackling tasks, solving puzzles, opening doors to secret lairs, and finding goals. As you gamify your situation, the primary impediment to achieving your goal becomes the challenge as you try to discover a way around it to go on.
- Points, leaderboards, badges, and awards can be used for positive feedback. For completing

little but significant tasks that help you reach your larger objective, points may be given. Badges are an excellent approach to provide yourself with immediate feedback.